Preparing Yourself for Your Child's Sex Education

LIN MYERS JOVANOVIĆ, PH.D.

Project Parent: Preparing Yourself for Your Child's Sex Education

Published by Plain Spoken Parenting

Editorial and Production Management: Janet Spencer King
www.spencerkingauthorservices.com
Cover and interior design: Karen Hudson

Printed in the United States of American for Worldwide Distribution
ISBN: 978-0-9978635-0-5

Praise for "Project Parent"

"There is a great need for comprehensive sex education for children, especially by parents. This unique book is a wonderful resource to help them take on that role. The author shows empathy for parents' anxieties and discomfort while being positive and encouraging about helping them meet this challenge. She guides adults in becoming aware of their own history and vulnerabilities about sex, which is enormously helpful in freeing them to be sex educators for their children. The information that provides quality sex education for special needs children is also impressive. Overall, the book is a valuable resource for adults who want to be positive models and sex educators for their children."

—Barry McCarthy, PhD, author, professor, workshop presenter

"I highly recommend this book for all parents who struggle with how and when to talk to their kids about sex. It helps parents identify aspects of their own experiences and upbringing that may hinder their attempts to communicate with their children. And it gives them information about how to overcome these barriers."

—Kate Shaw, PsyD, Licensed Clinical Psychologist

"Lin Myers Jovanović's book is an easy-to-read, comprehensive guide for parents to help them navigate the often awkward task of educating their children about sex. She covers all bases, including exercises for parents to deal with their anxieties and fears about doing it 'right.' She invites them to reflect on their own sexual journey, starting at a young age when curiosity about sex begins. As well, the author shares her personal experience teaching her own children about sex. I highly recommend this book to parents of all ages; as she point out, it is never too early to start to help children develop a mature and healthy attitude toward sex and sexuality."

—Barbara Desmarais, Parenting and Life Coach

"As a development couples counselor I marveled at the author's ability to design meaningful exercises for parents to foster teamwork as well as growth for each individual partner. These will help parents grow in their own sexual development and guide them in identifying their current parenting styles. The book's exercises also help parents learn ways to better communicate in general, which they can apply to all areas of their relationship. It is an impressive book that is rich with guidance and information."

—Kelly Scharver, LPC, Mom and Couples Counselor

"This aptly named book teaches how to handle the important and sensitive subject of children and sexuality. The author shares her knowledge and experience as a parent, researcher, and sex therapist. The book includes valuable information and many practical exercises that will help all parents conduct sex education for their children. It is a great source of wisdom and knowledge and a must have for parents everywhere."

—Charlotta Löfgren-Mårtenson, PhD, Director Centre for Sexology and Sexuality Studies, Malmö University

Acknowledgments

The idea of this book came from my work with parents who often expressed their concerns about how to begin the conversation with their children about tough topics like sex. I am indebted to them for showing me where they most needed help.

I am grateful to the many colleagues and students who have helped and encouraged me about this book especially Susan Goodwyn, who supported my dream from the beginning. I also want to express my gratitude to Tara Lain, who conducted her thesis work on parents' comfort with talking to their children about sex. My thanks as well to the Master Mentoring group led by the amazing Ellyn Bader, PhD, and Peter Pearson, PhD, of the Couples Institute. The group members have been my bedrock with ideas, support, and love as I navigated the many difficult parts of writing this book. I appreciate you all beyond words.

I owe a debt of gratitude to a number of people who looked at various drafts of the manuscript and contributed their ideas: Leanne Jacobson, Lexie Lee, Nicole Pallios, Dr. Alex Iantaffi, Megan Mooneyham Williamson, and Sarah Kiehl. Their feedback helped shape it into an accessible resource for parents.

I now fully understand why authors thank their editors. My deep thanks goes to Janet Spencer King, my editor, for her firm but kind hand in turning my writing into accessible content for parents. Her expertise has been invaluable.

Dedication

This book is dedicated to my children, Tiffany Macias, Ashlie Myers, Celeste Myers Gray, and Logan Bowers, who chose me to be their mother and have taught me to be a better person. And to my husband, Branislav Jovanović, whose support and love helped make this dream come true.

Contents

Introduction

What in the world do I say to my kids about sex?

Most of us grew up in a world where sexuality and the specifics about intimate relationships were a mystery. That's pretty amazing given all the information out there in the world about sex and relationships. Yet, parents in the 21st century are still unsure when and how to start sex education with their children and are resigned to all of it being scary and awkward.

As a sex educator, researcher, and therapist for over 25 years, I have seen firsthand the pain, awkwardness, and consequences of people who felt lost in navigating sex and relationships. I wrote this book specifically to help parents get beyond the pain, to feel prepared, and to deliver their values and accurate knowledge with confidence to their children. Plus there's a bonus: parents will become much more comfortable about their own sexual relationships.

I didn't become a mother until I was 44 years old. Because I had an infertility problem I eventually had to decide if I would adopt. At the time I was single, but I determined that I needed to act on this now. I ended up bringing two sisters, then ten and eleven years old, into my home. They had come from a difficult background and I knew raising them would be a challenge.

Even as a sex researcher and educator for so many years, I was somewhat unprepared for the first instance of how sexuality popped up in our lives. As I was folding clothes one day, the girls ran in from the park at the end of our block, burst into the room, and asked me what a blowjob was. Luckily, I had my face turned away from them and had a moment to take a deep breath. I was able first to calmly ask them where they had heard that term and they explained that an older boy at the park had said it. Now, this was when the Clinton impeachment trial was going on and the term blowjob was out there in public in a way it had never been before. With another deep breath, I said, "That is when a person puts his or her mouth on the genitals of another person for pleasure." The girls looked at each other, said "ew," and ran back out to play.

I was exhausted from just that one brief conversation! I was glad I had the presence of mind to ask them where they had heard this and I followed it up by quickly walking to the park to find the 15-year-old who was the culprit. In no uncertain terms I explained to him that if he wanted to talk about things like that again, it had better not be to my girls.

In that experience I was confronted fully with many things about being a parent: how I would respond to questions out of the blue, what I would actually say to my kids, and how I would need to protect them in this world. My extensive education in aspects of human sexuality certainly helped me, but it didn't prepare me for the challenges of parenting my own children.

My purpose in this book is to help coach parents in how

to navigate the various ways their children's sexual and relational selves will emerge as they grow up. No matter the age of their children now, parents can start today to build a bridge that will open up conversations with them about their bodies and their connections to others.

Parents have a variety of concerns about this part of their parenting. Are these some of yours?

- I won't know what to say
- I don't know the right time to begin
- I don't know enough about the topic
- My partner wants me to do this alone or he or she will be upset with me if I speak about sex to our children
- The kids might ask me about my sex life or my relationship
- What if they talk to their friends about what we've talked about?
- I don't know what is appropriate to discuss with my daughter vs. my son

You will learn in Step 1 of this book that children's sexuality and the desire to connect with others begins at birth and continues to unfold over the years. You might be surprised to learn that research has shown as children grow, they *want* their parents to be their primary source of information about sex and relationships. They may not always be receptive to these types of conversations, but they want that connection with you; they want to learn about your values and they want to feel safer to go into the world of relationships and sexuality.

Past experience often leads to beliefs and attitudes that also keep parents from educating their children. Are these some of yours?

- I'll be too anxious to talk with my kids or answer their questions
- If I talk to them about sex too early they will go out and experiment
- It's against my religion to talk about these things
- Talking about sex will scare the children
- It is the mother's job
- We will all be too embarrassed
- The kids aren't old enough yet to know about these things
- Is the right time to talk with them about sex when they start asking questions?

Life is full of events that make parents anxious or reactive. In Step 2 you will learn techniques for overcoming your fears and anxieties. Research shows that giving children an ongoing sex education has some powerful effects: children taught this way engage in sexual behaviors at an older age than average; they are much less likely to get pregnant or get someone pregnant, and they are also much less likely to contract an sexually transmitted disease (STD.) These are important reasons to provide your child with ongoing and meaningful information about sex and relationships! Another surprise for parents is discovering what their religious tradition actually has to say about the topic of sexuality rather than just assuming knowledge about it. I will help you explore your experiences and beliefs in Steps 3 and 4.

Few people have actually examined what their values are regarding sex and relationships. Step 5 is designed to help parents clarify their values about the many aspects of these topics. This step will prepare you to talk with your partner or co-parent, as well as consider what and how you want to share those values with your children.

Parents may find they don't agree about whose job it is or who should talk to which child. They may have conflicting values and beliefs. Wouldn't you like to be able to talk these things through with your mate and reach some common ground? Step 6 is all about teaming up with your co-parent to explore this important area of parenting.

The next step is designed to fill in those educational gaps everyone has, from what topics are age-appropriate to the basic facts about sexuality and relationships. Step 7 provides a rich resource to guide parents in their own education.

The last two Steps, 8 and 9, discuss proven methods for positive nonverbal and verbal communication. Parents will find that the ways in which they approach their children and how they respond to the kids play a role in improving connections in all areas of family life. Talking about almost any difficult topic becomes a manageable part of parenting. Your children will thank you for this!

I've added two chapters at the end of this book to address special issues in some families. In an age where divorce and blended families are common, parenting gets even more complicated. Extended family members may have their own attitudes, beliefs, and approaches that conflict with yours. Additionally, there are a number of other people in your children's lives, including perhaps day-care workers, school personnel and medical staff, just to name a few. Chapter 10 describes ways to more effectively engage these people who make up your village in raising your child.

Another situation in which parenting about sex and relationships can get especially complicated is in families with children who do not fit the societal norm. The areas I discuss are when a child has a mental illness; a developmental disability; is on the autism spectrum; lives with a congenital or acquired medical condition; has a history of abuse or trauma; is gender nonconforming, or comes out as gay while growing up. These factors alone can create very different challenges for parents, and it's tempting to put sex and relationship education aside. It would be a big mistake to do so, as you will learn. In Chapter 11 you will find many resources and suggestions for how you can incorporate appropriate sex and relationship education for your child, whatever the situation.

Are you ready to prepare yourself for these crucial areas of parenting? This book will be your guide.

CHAPTER 1

Step 1:
When Sexuality Education Should Begin

"Curiosity will conquer fear even more
than bravery will."
—James Stephens

Sexuality is a natural and integral part of being a human being. Indeed, we are born sexual creatures and we remain so until we die. However, I find that many people are resistant to this idea. The most common reason I see is confusion about the meaning of sexuality. For example, are we talking about genetic sex (being labeled as male or female); physical activities we refer to as "having sex"; body parts we call sex organs, or the sex drive, i.e. engaging in certain behaviors? Let's take a look to find out what, exactly, sexuality is.

In the field of human sexuality, prominent researchers Hilber and Colombini write that sexuality encompasses a wide swath including: "... sex, gender identities and roles, sexual orientation, eroticism, pleasure, intimacy and reproduction." Furthermore, they continue, people experience and express their sexuality in "... thoughts, fantasies, desires, beliefs, attitudes, values, behaviors, practices, roles and relationships." You may be relieved to read that the researchers do qualify this list, explaining that although sexuality can be all of the above, people don't necessarily experience or express all of them.

Although the issue of sexuality gets complicated, I like to use that word as the overarching term rather than "sex," which is often substituted for it. It's my preference because the concept of sexuality includes everything parents need to consider in educating their children. Not only that, given the central role sexuality plays in the human experience, I firmly believe it is important to start educating children about sexuality from birth.

I would bet that some of you are shaking your head about now. After all, you are no doubt thinking, a baby can't possibility understand things like that. But consider this – sexuality is woven into our lives from the beginning. Given the magnitude of the definition above of human sexuality, we know that it affects our children's health, their relationships, how they attach to others, how they learn aspects of language, and how they become part of the world. And all of these are involved in how we educate children beginning at birth! To put this in context, in the following pages I briefly explain how sexuality emerges in human beings.

An Age Guide to Sexual Development

The human body responds with physical expressions of sexuality even before birth as ultrasound images have revealed erections in male fetuses. During the first year of life, boy babies experience spontaneous erections and girls lubricate. Just as infants wave their arms and legs around as part of their development, their genitals also function without any apparent 'sexual' input. It is simply a natural part of being a human being. Up until the age of about three to four, it is not uncommon for both girls and boys to masturbate and appear to find pleasure and even experience a release that looks like an orgasm.

Children sometimes use their hands to explore their genitals, or they may rock rhythmically against pillows, toys, or other objects. They tend to masturbate in this way during times of boredom or as a way to relieve stress. Again, this is a natural human response that does not involve any kind of external sexual stimulation. It is not uncommon for parents to see their children touch themselves in public or to hear from childcare providers that this has happened (often at nap time). Parents typically do try to do something about these behaviors and this, too, is sex education. We will explore this in depth in later chapters

A second important emergence of sexuality in early childhood has to do with the formation of gender identity. Until quite recently, people determined gender based on the appearance of a newborn's genitals. Today we recognize that gender identity and expression is not only biological but that it has a psychological part as well, including being shaped by societal experiences. Research shows that parents influence their children's expression of what it means to be masculine or feminine from birth. A long-ago study observed parents and their newborn in the first 24 hours of life; researchers asked parents to describe their baby on such things as their physical movement or the duration and loudness of their cries. The study also included a group of independent observers to rate them who were blind as to whether babies were boys or girls. Interestingly, the independent observers found no significant differences in how the babies behaved while parents were quite likely to say that boys were more physically active or that their cries were stronger than the girls.

When children reach age three, their sense of themselves as male or female generally becomes more apparent to the world. Furthermore, at this point children can usually say whether they are a girl or a boy, although they do not have a deeper understanding of what this means until they are a bit older. Their body image is forming at this time as well, which can affect their sense of self in both childhood and adult relationships.

As children go into preschool and kindergarten, social factors continue to shape gender identity. They take in stereotypes and expectations of being a male or female, which to an extent are shaped by the expectations of those in their social circle. I say to an extent because some children may assert themselves to be the opposite of what their genetic sex and physical appearance would indicate. I don't want to get into specifics about this, only to point out that while gender identity is generally considered to be fully formed around the age of 3, since psychological and social factors can affect it, parents do well to learn more about it as part of parenting young children. (We will explore your own meaning of gender identity and your values around male and female roles more fully in a later chapter.)

Preschool-age children are naturally curious and want to explore. Many kids like to run around without all their clothes on, and they may be interested in what other kids look like. Although this curiosity can catch parents off-guard, it is also part of sexuality education. As kids get to be about four or five they may be bolder in their interests. Here is where parents might find them playing doctor or trying to peek into parents' bedroom while they are dressing or sneak ing to see something on TV or the Internet. Once into and past first grade kids might mimic behaviors with their same-aged friends that they see in older kids and adults, such as lying down next to each other and talking, handholding, or even kissing. Children in the tween years, (8-12) anticipating how their bodies will change as they grow older, may become more private and possibly even sneaky about their curiosity and exploration, but it is likely still happening. You can see that even if you thought children wouldn't need sex education much before puberty, they are pretty brilliant at creating sex education on their own.

Puberty Starts

Puberty begins a little earlier for girls than boys; parents can expect to see hormonal maturation and its resulting signs of physical change around age nine or ten for girls and around age twelve for boys. Early signs for girls are breast bud development and in boys, enlargement of the testicles. More obvious physical changes, known as secondary sex characteristics, will begin to develop after this including pubic and armpit hair, menses, penis enlargement, height, voice and weight changes, and muscular development.

Increased sexual feelings accompany changes in sex and adrenal hormone levels in boys and girls, as is greater awareness of the world brought about by changes in sensitivity to sights, smells, touch, hearing, and painful stimuli. As a rule, children begin to become more aware of who they are physically and emotionally attracted to just before or during active pubertal changes. Clearly we will have a lot to talk about concerning the period of puberty!

Education Advantages

Educating yourself to gain as much factual information about sexuality as possible will benefit you and your children in many ways. Among others, you will help your children develop a correct vocabulary about sexuality terminology making it more comfortable to talk about it; you can provide more accurate information, and most importantly, you will be opening up crucial lines of communication that will increase family closeness and help protect your children from sexual abuse, whether in childhood, adolescence, or beyond. Educated parents are less likely to punish their children's developmentally normal sexual behaviors, which not only leads to more effective family communication, but also to more positive sexual decision-making in their children.

Parents of tweens or teenagers should not despair that it is too late to put the information in this book to good use. In fact it will help you open lines of communication no matter the age of your children. As is true of all of life – none of us can change what we did before, but we can change what we do from this day forward.

In the next chapter I will explain some of the common emotional reactions to scary situations and introduce you to helpful ways to self-soothe.

CHAPTER 2

Step 2:
Overcoming Fears and Expectations

"And one has to understand that braveness is not the absence of fear but rather the strength to keep on going forward despite the fear." —Paulo Coelho

People rightly fear certain parenting duties. Talking with kids about sex is right up there at the top of the list. Faced with embarrassment and fear, parents say their children are too young or they will wait until the child brings the topic up. Advice to parents is frequently a 'just get over it' command or a 'find the right time suggestion'. These approaches don't work. In this chapter I will show why the body and mind respond in ways that creates fear or blocks effective behavior and then I introduce three techniques to reduce or eliminate these unhelpful emotional responses.

Core Body Reactions

Fear is a natural human emotion. It is there to protect the body especially if it is in immediate danger. The word fear comes from Old English meaning danger or sudden calamity or peril. When confronted by a real danger bodies mobilize to fight off the threat. Take a near miss in a car on the highway. The sympathetic nervous system goes into action. Eyes dilate to take in the scene, blood pumps to the muscles to control the car, and people feel their hands sweating and their mouth go dry. Quick action avoids the danger.

Reactions of the sympathetic nervous system to danger are mostly automatic. The body's action may be to fight, to flee, or to freeze. Humans are genetically programmed to survive and their bodies do lots of responding without any help from their brains. When the danger is gone, people are more aware that their arms and legs still tremble, their heart is beating hard, and their breath is labored. The body will tingle as the effects take time to ebb away.

People can learn to temper the automatic responses of their bodies to fear, but it is normal to feel a pounding heart or experience sweaty palms in a tense situation. I want parents to wisely accept that waiting until they experience no unpleasant bodily reactions before they act is not realistic.

Temperament and Learned Responses

Some people come from families who are sensitive to light, more introverted or extroverted, from people who might like their environment to be specifically neat and tidy, or who like to stay up late at night. These qualities are referred to as temperament or personality and considered mainly inborn parts of people that influence behavior. People readily use temperament or personality labels for themselves such as early bird, easy going, distractible, high energy, happy-go-lucky, or sensitive.

Characteristics like these appear during the early years of life and stay pretty stable as people get older. However, a person is not absolutely stuck with their genetic endowment when it comes to interacting with the world. Sometimes a person will discover that certain labels don't fit for them anymore. On the other hand, even if someone is a shy or especially private person they can learn ways to honor themselves and their desire to give their best as a parent. It isn't necessary for parents to change their personality so they can talk with their children about sex. This book will help people know themselves better and find easier and more effective ways to get the job of parenting done.

People also learn to label their experiences as positive or negative. Throughout life they become conditioned to perceive certain situations as scary or as a threat, whether that is the reality or not. Anticipating something unpleasant may also trigger fear or, more mildly, anxiety. When Pavlov described training a dog to salivate to the sound of a bell, called the conditional response, it wasn't that the dog wanted to eat the bell. Instead the dog had become conditioned to associate that sound with the food he was given. Once the brain labels something as positive, people look forward to that experience and even seek it out because they have learned to expect that a specific reward will occur following a certain cue.

Conditioned action can be a useful response for some situations, such as moving out of a roadway when a car coming. However, people can also learn to label even harmless situations as negative and when this happens they end up putting a lot of conscious and unconscious effort into avoidance of those situations and associated emotions. For example, humans respond appropriately to a loud sound used to scare them. When a person sneaks up and yells 'Boo' when another person is not expecting it, predictable things happen. A scream escapes and the body shrinks away from the threat. Some people like a good scare and can laugh it away, while others take a long time to get over it. Being repeatedly scared and teased to get over it can train the brain to automatically take over and to become fearful of any potential scary situation. Now the body's natural reaction to protect has become associated with a specific cue or situation and gets generalized to perceived threats. This is how people learn to fear things that can't actually hurt them.

Learning Negative Cues

The responses of others (laughing, name calling, shaming) also become connected to the event and people avoid situations where their natural responses could be triggered again. Children are curious and ask their parents about where babies come from. They are curious about their bodies and the bodies of other children. The parent's facial expression, tone of voice, and specific words in response to questions and actions will condition the child. These experiences are carved into the brain of the child. Negative cues and punishment teach the child to avoid the question or behavior, while positive cues and behavior teach the child that their parents are safe and their curiosity is acceptable. Even before children form language they experience emotions and learn about their world. Such learning is deep and important.

Negative cues can unconsciously trigger the part of memory about oneself. Autobiographical memories come back to us in a flash and are sharply felt. People may not have language for some things that they learned early in life, but the body remembers and reacts. Now, the great thing about being more aware of fears and reactions is that these conditioned responses can be changed. Just reading this book may cause some people to have negative reactions and to experience unpleasant emotions. That automatic reaction tells them it isn't safe to move forward. They can't 'just get over it'. This second step is to learn the automatic thoughts and emotional reactions that block desired action and to uncover self-soothing techniques that work best for a given person. By practicing different ways to self-soothe people can heal the parts of themselves that harbor fear, embarrassment, and shame around the topic of sex and learn to manage the natural anxiety that comes with difficult topics.

Steps to Self-Soothing

It is normal for parents to feel scared or embarrassed about beginning sex education with their children. A first important action for our work together is to simply accept whatever feelings or thoughts arise. People can beat themselves up for having negative reactions. This is a waste of time. As the quote at the beginning of this chapter points out, we may not eliminate fear completely, but we can gain the courage to keep moving forward.

Awareness and acceptance from where a person starts are powerful first steps to getting ready for change. The act of simply accepting feelings and thoughts is not necessarily easy. Because fear and anxiety can get triggered to meet the goals of educating children about sex, learning ways to calm these emotions is important. Self-soothing techniques help people counteract negative thoughts and emotional responses that they may have picked up along the way, even unconsciously. They are a way to substitute a positive experience or reaction for a negative one. Some people find that prayer or meditation helps them be more present and calm in the moment, others may use physical exercise to release fears, and others may use healthy (or unhealthy) ways to distract themselves.

Many times people try to push away feelings by saying they aren't right or that they are silly or too unpleasant. Attempting to do this can take tremendous energy and if done for too long leads to more stress, anxiety, and even fear. The body can't work well with those kinds of constant stressors and they may cause emotional and physical consequences such as trouble sleeping, heightened anxiety, or even depression. This can lead people to act in ways that are truly against their own best interest: avoiding any risk, procrastinating, arguing, etc. To counteract these kinds of negative physical and emotional effects, we can practice self-soothing methods and become calmer and more effective.

I find it interesting in my work that parents can readily teach their children how to self-soothe, perhaps to go to sleep at night or when something upsetting happens in their world, but they don't apply the same principles to themselves. Now is your time to apply these good parenting skills to yourself.

Counteracting Disempowering Thoughts

This first self-soothing technique is a way to identify and replace disempowering thoughts and reactions with empowering ones. In his clinical work, Albert Ellis saw that people told themselves things that simply weren't rational (e.g., I should have been able to do that job no matter what!) and that the combination of these irrational thoughts paired with negative emotional responses (intensive frustration, fear or anger) kept his clients stuck. All that needed to happen was the irrational thought and a cascade of negative emotions and anxiety-related body reactions (racing heart) would lead to continued inappropriate or ineffective action. Further, he found people made things worse by beating themselves up for getting stuck. Ellis developed Rational Emotive Behavioral Therapy (REBT) to show people a rational and effective way of replacing negative thoughts and feelings, which leads to appropriate emotional and physical responses and achieving of one's goals. This is the amazing power of the mind.

A main goal here could be to be able to give children accurate and appropriate sex education as they grow up. The first activity is to ponder that goal and make a list of the irrational or disempowering thoughts or beliefs about that goal. Then the person identifies negative emotions associated with those thoughts or beliefs. Any bothersome physical reactions are noted. Now the person can clearly see the pattern that is getting in their way. Next, specific types of self-defeating thoughts are identified: A command or demand ("I should", "I must not"); An event viewed as unbearable (I'd just die"); Catastrophizing or 'awfulizing' (The worst thing, It would be terrible); or name-calling (I'm an idiot).

The next step in changing the brain, and ultimately behavior, is to create some rational or empowering phrases that can be used to actively counteract negative cues and disempowering thoughts. Then, the person actively practices replacing self-defeating beliefs and reactions with positive and empowering thoughts and reactions.

Here is an example of this technique in action:

Typical thoughts:

- I shouldn't be embarrassed or afraid.
- It would be the worst to talk about where babies come from!
- Maybe talking about sex is too much for them.
- What if they ask me something I don't know? I'm hopeless on this topic!

Underlying self-defeating beliefs:

- I <u>must</u> not let myself be embarrassed
- I absolutely <u>can't stand it</u>
- It will <u>harm</u> my children to know certain things
- I'm an <u>idiot</u> for not knowing what to say

Emotional responses:

- Scared
- Mortified
- Self-conscious
- Shamed
- Avoidant

Notice the statements command a person not to think or feel certain ways. Most people get stressed out and exhausted if they think this way. Their automatic protective body responses get triggered to try to manage the anxiety and stress. Their thinking keeps them in an endless loop of fear, self-recrimination, and more disempowering thoughts and feelings. The next steps offer a way out of this loop. Taking one or two irrational thoughts, the person creates some empowering thoughts that can be used to dispute their current core beliefs that get in their way.

Typical irrational thoughts:

- I will be too embarrassed to talk about how babies are made. I can't show my kids I don't have all the answers or they will lose all respect for me.

Disputing and Empowering thoughts:

- Maybe I will be embarrassed to talk with my children about how babies are born, but that won't really be the end of the world.

- If I don't have all the answers I can look them up or get some help. My kids will respect me more for admitting I don't know everything.

- It is okay for me to be human and not have all the answers. The universe, God, my family love and respect me the way I am.

- A little embarrassment won't kill me and I prefer feeling that to not preparing my children for happy, healthy, and respectful sexual experiences.

The list can be tailored to a particular person's list of disempowering thoughts and beliefs. The last major step is to repeat the disempowering thought and follow up with the empowering thought. It is a conversation with self that disputes what has come to be the truth and replaces it with a rational and helpful statement. Most people find that they feel more and more relieved as they practice the technique. Unconscious or conscious thoughts and reactions that drive avoidance, anger, or fear are confronted and the antidote is applied – the rational thought. Retraining the brain and behavior is possible.

Tame By Tapping

One of my favorite ways to self-soothe and change automatic reactions involves consciously connecting mind and body. This technique is largely borrowed from the Emotional Freedom Technique (EFT) and involves acknowledging thoughts and feelings, as well as practicing empowering thoughts while tapping on the body. Tapping can be practiced almost anywhere. A person can think about any stressful thing they might be facing that day or in life and apply this technique. With a particular thought in mind, maybe having some conversations about sex with their child or co-parent, the goal is to first allow awareness of what emotions or thoughts surface without judgment or any attempts to push them away. This may take some practice because people are conditioned to stay away from unpleasant feelings or thoughts. A specific phrase or labeling of that person's bodily reaction comes to mind such as, "I feel scared when I think about talking with my children about sex." We ask the person to give an intensity rating between 1 and 10. Picking something with a rating of at least 5 will allow for the person to notice a change. Next, to become centered the person takes a couple of deep breaths. Just a few cycles of deep breathing can result in a release of some of the tension they feel in their shoulders or other parts of their body. Next, using the fingers of one hand, they begin to tap on the outer palm of the other hand, the karate chop point as it is called, and repeat a phrase like one of these below, beginning with the phrase, "Even though...":

- Even though I feel stressed (overwhelmed, scared) when I think about talking with my child about sexuality, I accept my feelings and myself.
- Even though now I can't imagine talking with my child (or partner) about sexuality, I accept my feelings and love myself.
- Even though I think bad things could happen to my children if I talk with them about sexuality, in this moment I accept my thoughts and myself.

Rather than attempting to push away feelings and thoughts, the person attempts as best he or she can to name what those feelings and thoughts actually are. Breathing deeply a few times slows them down and allows them to stay in the moment. The use of the phrase "Even though" is an important step in accepting and acknowledging self. It can also feel good for some people to include some mention of their spiritual beliefs in their acceptance statements (for example, "and I know God loves me as I am" or "I know the universe accepts me as I am"). A person's self-soothing thoughts and actions are crucial here to changing and calming negative thoughts and emotions, reducing stress and worry, and eliminating blocks.

The phrase or phrases are repeated a number of times while continuing to tap so that mind and body more fully connect. Most people start to feel that intensity level drop just a little bit more. To continue changing the mind and body, I would now direct the person to note if anything else came up and to continue to tap, acknowledge those thoughts as well, and even gently ask themselves what those thoughts are all about.

Another step is to then ask the person to include some empowering thoughts and continue tapping. They could be something like these:

- I do know more than my children do. I can confidently talk with them about sex.
- It is kind of silly to be so afraid. I have faced scarier things and been able to face my fears.
- I can get more information and help to have these kinds of talks with my children.
- I don't have to do this alone. My partner and I can take turns when it comes to talking about sex.

Expanded tapping techniques can be found on the Internet. Creating more empowering thoughts to repeat will also help. After breathing, admitting fears, and tapping while repeating empowering phrases it is time to check back in regarding the intensity of emotion that is present now. Generally, most people will find they have a significant drop in their rating. Continued practice can lead to even greater reduction in disempowering thoughts and reactions.

The tapping itself may seem a bit funny, but it is an important part. Simply stating phrases can be helpful, but many people can still stay stuck in their heads or become overly focused on disempowering reactions such as numbing out, being avoidant, or blocking attention to the present. There are a variety of websites on the Internet that show extended procedures for tapping on the body. Tapping will affect those parts of the brain that that are there to protect the person in that assumption that they are in danger. These resources are available for the reader in a subsequent chapter. Parents can use tapping as a way to stay more connected to themselves while retraining their brains and bodies. This will lead to more connection and comfort with their children.

Grounding Techniques

Another method for bringing people fully into awareness is called grounding. Some people like to think of this as getting a solid foundation or connecting with the earth (thinking about sending out roots to be strongly attached to the earth) while others may like the idea of electrical grounding, whereby we can discharge too much built up brain activity.

Just as with tapping, the main focus here is on awareness of self. Grounding can be achieved in many ways; sitting, standing, dancing, walking, speaking, using the sight and touch of comforting objects, or mindfully listen to a song. Here is a popular method I use to teach grounding.

1. Find a quiet spot and sit in a chair with your feet squarely on the floor. Focus on how your feet are connected to the ground.
2. Imagine your toes gently gripping the earth, growing into the earth to provide you with a solid and secure foundation. Feel the energy that has previously built up and blocked you gently draining out through your feet and into the earth.
3. Now take your attention from the strong, calm foundation you have created in your feet upward through your legs; stay aware of how your legs keep your body erect, focusing on the strength of your thighs and the blood flowing through your muscles.
4. Continuing up the body, focus awareness on how your buttocks connects to the chair; experience how solidly your body is connecting to itself and the earth.
5. Become aware of how the chair connects with your back, the gentle support the chair gives you and how it encourages more grounding. Allow your head to sit easily on your shoulders so it can bob up and down as your shoulder muscles relax.

The energy and connection you have now established with your body will allow you to enjoy greater awareness of your being. Breathe deeply, bringing in oxygen and focus on how your circulation is taking that vital substance and giving life throughout your body. Your connection to the ground is now draining away any remaining anxiety and pent up energy you have been carrying.

Identifying Effective Self-Soothing

Parents can't 'just' get over their feelings and thoughts about talking with their kids about sexuality. Everyone needs help to overcome fears and to act in the healthiest way possible. This chapter has been focused on helping parents to get deeper down into the thoughts and feelings that actively block them from talking with there loved ones about sexuality. I want you to identify one or two ways that work best for you, be that grounding, tapping, replacing disempowering thoughts, praying, meditating, or exercising. Practice all of them and see which of them helps lower the intensity of emotion rating as much as possible. I will be encouraging you to use your techniques as we move through the rest of the steps.

CHAPTER 3

Step 3:
Knowing Your Story

"In youth we learn; in age we understand."
—Marie von Ebner-Eschenbach

Children are learning from the moment of birth and before the acquisition of language, making memories nonverbal and unconscious. Whether they learned to experience the world as a safe place or not was created through interactions with parents and others. What people learn directs what they do, consciously and unconsciously. Skip forward to being a parent. Automatic reactions to children's needs and behavior, positive or negative, will come as a surprise for many. For others there will be sharp selected memories of how they learned or the realization they just did something their parents had done they swore they would never do. Usually, only parts of the story of why these things happen are really known. Step Three is about exploring your own story in more depth, filling in the blanks, and becoming a more conscious parent. To begin, let's look first at how early connections are made.

Development of the Social Self and Attachment

Every human infant is born with core needs. Survival depends on connecting with others, so infants must attune to their caretakers to get those core needs met. This connection is called attachment and there are three main styles - secure, preoccupied, and avoidant. These are based on how the parents respond, interact, and connect to their young children and these styles predict how the child will respond to parents and others in their world. In adulthood, attachment style is found to affect how people form relationships and their beliefs about whether others can be counted on. Attachment style can make or break relationships.

Securely attached children have parents who are more present and in tune with their emotions, who encourage independent and shared exploration, and who show a measure of comforting physical connection. The children frequently seek connection with their parents and are easily comforted when events change their world. Secure attachment is estimated occur in about 50% of people.

In adult life, securely attached people are described as having developed a positive sense of themselves and a positive sense of others in the world; as being both valued and self-reliant as well as thinking the best of others. They can better balance being close and being independent or autonomous in the world because they have learned from their parents that core needs will likely be met.

When Attachment Isn't Secure

In contrast, parents who are not consistent, who are intrusive, or who look to their child for reassurance will teach them that the world is not a safe or reliable place. Preoccupied attachment results in children who are unwilling to explore the environment and who clings to the parent in most situations. They exhibit anxiety and anger at the parent after a normal separation and cannot be easily comforted. Internally, a negative sense of self develops, but an overly positive or overvaluing view of others is found. This type of anxious attachment is estimated to occur in about 20% of the population.

Overvaluing others, even with contrary evidence, results in adults who are clingy, preoccupied with their partner's every move, and who drive others away by demands for attention and approval. Yet, even with appropriate responses from others, Preoccupied folks are never satisfied or soothed, but they are driven to keep trying.

About 25% of the population falls in the insecure attachment style of Avoidant. Their parents are generally not physically expressive with them and they expect children to explore the environment on their own. They appear to try to sidestep the emotions of their children and if they are distressed, the parent expects them to comfort themselves. In learning to fend for themselves these children come to believe that they don't need others. They see themselves as positive and others as decidedly negative (can't be counted on). Avoidantly attached children often shut off any facial expression and appear detached from their world.

Even though a deep human part of the avoidant adult wants to connect with others, they are seen as dismissive, unemotional, and untouchable in their relationships. An inflated sense of self and an exaggerated independence develops to protect that human part of themselves.

Development of the Sexual Self

Development of the sexual self also begins at birth. We saw how babies touch themselves and get pleasure from that. Healthy touch from others also shapes our emotional selves and physical selves. Sexual responses such as lubrication or erection are instinctual, but sexual acts of humans are not 'natural' in the sense that they are instinctually produced and invariant in their execution, as we see in other animals. People learn about sexuality from family, friends, and culture as well as their own personal trial and error experiences with others. Some of this learning could be positive or painful. In adult life most people have either forgotten or never really considered how their sexuality was learned and shaped. The rest of this step is devoted to a series of exercises that will help you get clearer about your own history.

EXERCISE REMINDER

SUSPEND JUDGEMENT
STAY FOCUSED
SELF-SOOTHE

Exercise: Sexuality and Relationship Lifeline

PURPOSE: Creating a lifeline of experiences is a powerful way to jog memory and discover your learning and experiences. By seeing the roots of their story, people can understand why they behave the way they do. Difficult or stuck places can be identified. Positive experiences can be celebrated.

HOW TO: Your sexuality and relationship lifelines can be done separately or together. Do what works best for you. If you do them separately, you can combine them at the end to see how they overlap.

- Aim for an hour for each lifeline. Be prepared that you may have emotional responses to what you write. If you don't, that is also fine.
- Find a quiet place and do the exercise alone. Privacy and quiet will allow the mind to release memories.
- Use a blank piece of paper, preferably legal-size, and place it horizontally on your table. A pencil allows for corrections.
- Draw a horizontal line across the center of the paper. The left is your birthdate and the right is your current age. Think of your first conscious memory and mark it on your line with a brief description of the event. Put positive events above the line and negative ones below it. An event may be both positive and negative for you.
- You can move chronologically or stick things in as you remember them. Give yourself space for spontaneous recall.

Sexuality Lifeline

Below are some examples of typical life experiences that can influence your sexuality. Feel free to add any others that have meaning for you.

Typical experiences:

- curiosity about others
- sexual play with self or others
- awareness of your gender and/or any gender conflicts
- memories of first sexual feelings
- the topic of sex (or reproduction, etc.)
- yourself as a sexual being
- first kiss
- first masturbation
- first time feeling turned on or first wet dream
- awareness of pregnancy and what it meant
- experiences of your parents talking with you about sex or sexual behavior
- school or religious instruction about sex
- first sexual experiences with another person (voluntary or not - you can separate them out on lifeline and make a note)
- medical exam - testicular or pelvic
- first orgasm
- wedding night

EXERCISE REMINDER

GIVE YOURSELF TIME
ALLOW MEMORIES TO EMERGE
ACCEPT WHAT YOU REMEMBER

- other notable sexual experiences

After you have entered your experiences on the lifeline, do the following:

- Add more detail if you like
- List who was there
- Note the context
- Identify emotional experiences (pleasure, pain, anxiety, shame, empowerment etc.)

As an example, here is the start of my sexual lifeline as a list:

- FCM (age 2 ½) – a big black dog we had
- Peeking at parents as they changed clothes (age 5) (excited, interested)
- Playing doctor with my neighbor girlfriend (age 6) (curious)
- Hiding in the basement and laying on top of each other with the neighbor boy (age 9) (scared, excited, not sure what it all meant)
- Practice kissing with my girlfriend (age 11) (kissed with our mouths closed to see what it was like, not really turned on just curious)
- Hearing parents having sex (scared, wasn't sure what was happening, thought my dad was hurting my mom)
- 6th grade lecture on menstruation, reading the insert in the box of pads (weird experience to see the film and to imagine having to wear a pad)
- Seeing first Playboy magazine (age 12) (exciting, naughty, still didn't know what it all meant)

- Started my period (age 13) (excited, could now take private showers in PE)
- Told by my mother to shower more regularly (age 13) (embarrassed, hurt by the way she told me)
- First masturbation to orgasm (age 13) (pleasure, can't remember being told not to and no one said anything to me at this age)
- Allowed to go on a triple date with my sister and her friend and some older boys. Lots of making out in the theatre (age 14) (scared, turned on). This is when my Dad starting acting more weird about boys and warning me about what they wanted (whatever that was)

Relationship Lifeline

Now, using a new piece of paper if you choose, chart meaningful relationships across your entire life so far. These will include family, friends, neighbors, teachers, religious leaders, lovers, spouses, co-workers, close friends in adulthood, etc.

After you are through, identify the following:

- How you developed friendships growing up
- Best models of healthy relationships
- Friendships in your adult life
- Most important friendships/relationships
- Endings of friendships/relationships
- Significant emotional experiences (sadness, pain, anxiety, shame, happiness, etc.)

Putting It All Together

You now have your unique story. Normally people remember things they hadn't thought of for quite a while and both positive and negative emotions will surfaced. A much clearer picture of what you have learned that made you who you are emerges. You can now actively redirect negative experiences and scripts into positive action for your parenting.

Do the following:

- Growing up, outline who affected your sense of self as a person, a woman or man, and a sexual human being. Explore what you learned.
- List at least two important friendships before adulthood and briefly explain what about them was important to you.
- Name your most positive and most negative sexual experiences.
- Consider how your parents gave you sex education. What things do you want to keep and what do you want to leave behind? If you were brought up in a particular religious tradition, do the same thing.
- Make a list of any disempowering thoughts you learned about sex and relationships (sex is bad, other people can't be trusted) and note the source.

Applying Learning from Your Lifelines

There are several creative and healing ways to use the information from the lifeline exercises. With your list of disempowering thoughts you can go through the REBT procedure from the last chapter. Writing a narrative or chronicle of these life experiences can be empowering. You are the expert in your own life and taking a step to revisit all the important influences around sex and relationships can be helpful identifying your way forward.

Here is a bit of my story. My father was an important source of my sense of self as a person, a woman and a sexual being. He gave me many conflicting messages about men and what they wanted. He tried to control my sexuality by interrogating any boys I dated and asking them about their motives. The message was that sex was dangerous, mine and anyone else's. On the other hand, he told me I could become anything I wanted to be and encouraged me to go to college and beyond. Yet, there was also a lot of pressure in my family to define myself through marriage. This and more left me thinking that boys could be dangerous, but that they were also an important (virtually vital) part of how I was supposed to define myself. I was shamed into thinking I was too interested in sex and that if a man wanted me, that was my fault. I believed I was the problem, not the messages my family or the culture gave me.

When I did my own sexual lifeline years ago I could more clearly see the way my family, my society, and my experiences formed a narrative of me as the bad girl in the story. Now, I am a baby boomer, so there are likely to be some generational differences in my story for that reason. With help and using some of the techniques in this book, I was able to shift my view of myself, to separate my own unique being as valuable, and to sift through my own misconceptions. I could see myself not as a problem, but as a product of all I had experienced. I could forgive myself my hurtful behaviors to self and others, and use my story in something much more productive, like in my teaching and in writing this book. There is much to be gained through a respectful and no-blaming approach to ourselves.

Another application of these exercises in self-discovery is to prepare yourself for what you want to share with a loved one, a partner, or your children. Let's focus on children here. Kids are known to ask parents directly about their personal experience and some parents are fearful about this, which is why they may avoid any 'sex' talks. Whether you open the door or not, children will be curious, so let's consider how you want to set the ground rules now. First, I am here to tell you that you have a right to keep your private life private from your children. We may have made decisions in our teen or adult years that weren't using the best judgment. Details of your first sexual experience, your trauma history, or how you personally like to be touched is your business.

This again does not mean they won't be curious; just that you have the right to model that certain aspects of our lives can remain private.

As part of your preparation now you can look over your life experiences and make your own decision about what you would be willing to share, what you might be willing to share (maybe based on the age or your child or other factors), and what you absolutely will never share. The reasons are your own ("I just don't want to," "That's too embarrassing," or "It's none of their business!"). You don't have to justify yourself to anyone here and what you write in this column can be as short or long as you like. It is okay to have a private space of your own in your heart and mind. For any with sexual or relational trauma in our life, this is an important concept and part of healing.

Finally, you may choose to use your lifeline story to open up conversations with your significant other or spouse, a trusted friend, or a therapist. If you and your partner are working through this book together, sharing your lifeline can be a great way to move toward how you both will talk with your children, what you will talk about, and who will do the talking. Sharing this kind of information does take trust and it is wise to have an agreement about what details you will share and how you both will honor that information. I will cover more details about talking with your partner/co-parent in a subsequent chapter, so you may choose to wait until you have read that one.

Filling In the Blanks

Doing an exercise like the lifeline may have left you with some gaps in your story. As you are opening the door on understanding yourself better, I recommend talking with your parents, if they are still around, about their experiences when they were growing up. Typically, parents are a bit more open when their children are adults and when the topic isn't on specific sexual behavior. Knowing your family's history can also help you decide how to rewrite your current family's story. Siblings can also be a good source of information or you may want to talk to friends about what they experienced growing up.

CHAPTER 4

Step 4:
Digging Deeper

"There's nothing that can help you understand your beliefs more than trying to explain them to an inquisitive child." —Frank A. Clark

When parents communicate their knowledge, values, and expectations clearly and positively, their children are much more likely to engage in healthy and respectful sexual and relational behaviors. That is the good news. The not so good news is that parents aren't always clear about these things for themselves when that inquisitive child asks a question. Being unprepared can complicate an important part of parenting. In this step you will expand on what you discovered about yourself in Step 3 by digging into your specific learning about sex and relationships. Getting clear will make positive communication possible and much easier.

Personal Archeology

There are three parts to digging deeper. First is an exercise to identify what you learned about general aspects of sex and relationships. This is an extension of the lifeline exercise. The list of topics I have compiled will jog your memory and also help you think about areas you need to learn more about.

Second is an exploration of what specific beliefs you learned from your parents, religion, and culture. In the third part I guide you in putting it all together, and helping you continue to construct a clear direction for your own parenting.

Exercise: General Learning about Sex and Relationships

There are a wide variety of basic things people have learned and need to learn about their physical and relational selves. I have created a list of things children, teens, and young adults learn about sex and relationships that shape their behavior and interactions. Remember that this is a snapshot and it isn't important if you can't remember every detail. If I've left out something that is important to you, feel free to add it in.

PURPOSE: To identify what and when you specifically learned about the physical body and behavior and sex and relationships, as well as uncover the source. To identify areas where more learning needs to happen.

HOW TO: Take a piece of paper and for each numbered item on the list (see below), give a brief description of when, how, and from whom you learned about the item. It might look something like this:

What, When and from Whom Did I Learn About...

- Proper names for genitals
- What masturbation is
- How a female gets pregnant and has a baby
- Proper hygiene after puberty
- Good touch/bad touch
- Privacy for your own body/sexuality
- Differences between male and female bodies
- Gender (differences in male and female roles)
- How to cope with emotional changes/reactions
- Wet dreams (nocturnal emissions)
- How to be a good friend
- Menstruation
- Birth control methods
- Moral values about being sexually active
- Close relationships
- STDs/STIs (sexually transmitted diseases or infections)
- How to protect from getting and transmitting STDs/STIs
- Intercourse
- Oral sex
- Orgasm

- Same sex attraction (homosexuality)
- What dating is about
- Anal sex
- Pornography
- Abortion
- What characteristics to look for in a romantic partner
- Sexual coercion
- Violence in relationships
- Risks from using alcohol or other drugs
- Decision-making about being sexually active
- Monogamy/fidelity in a relationship
- How to handle rejection
- Sexual harassment
- What it means to give consent
- How to break up with someone
- Prostitution
- What rape means
- ... Add your own idea

For now, look over your list and circle any areas where you want to get more information. Now, let's apply what you've learned about yourself in the next part of your personal archeology. In the next exercise the focus is on particular sources of your information and what you learned before you left home. In the list below, parents (mother or father) refers to anyone who had primary responsibility to raise you. The term sex is used to cover any sexual acts.

Exercise: Digging A Little Deeper

PURPOSE: To see more clearly specific learning from family, friends, religion, and culture.

HOW TO: Below is a list of question stems for you to complete. Don't spend to long on any one stem, just write the first thing that comes into your mind.

- My father thought sex...
- The topic of masturbation....
- When I was growing up, my religion told me sex...
- My biggest fears about sex when I was young were....
- My mother thought sex...
- When I was rejected by a person I was interested in, my (mother, father, etc.) told me to....
- In my culture, sex is thought of as....
- I learned that my body...
- The topic of drugs and sex...
- If I tried to talk with my father about sex...
- In my culture, men...
- If someone tried to hurt me emotionally, my parent(s)...
- When I was allowed to start

EXERCISE REMINDER

WORK QUICKLY
CLARIFY YOUR SOURCES
CREATE YOUR PATH

dating, I was told...

- When I am dating someone, I was taught that sex should happen....
- My father told me that a man...
- My parent(s) taught me that violence within a relationship was....
- If I asked my mother about sex she...
- My parent(s) taught me that love...
- My mother told me that a woman....
- When in a relationship, my parent said being faithful was....
- I was taught that affection...
- If I ever had a scare about pregnancy or STDs, I talked with...
- When it comes to using protection against pregnancy or STDs, my parents said....
- My mother said a man...
- Girls that were sexually active were thought of as...
- In my culture, women...
- Virginity....
- My parent(s) taught me that homosexuality...
- Sex within a relationship is...
- In my family, we never talked about sex because...
- The person I went to if I had a question about sex was...
- Somebody who got an STD or got pregnant was thought of as...

Add in any other thoughts you have to the list. Now, going back over your list you can start to see further specific messages regarding what your family, culture, or religion thought about specific topics like gender roles, relationship values, certain sexual behaviors, etc. Your picture of your sex and relationship education should be much clearer now.

Putting It All Together

Looking over your answers in the first and second exercises, put a plus sign for positive experience or messages, a minus sign for negative ones, and an N for the neutral ones. You can consider some of the following questions:

- What are the positive aspects of your learning you want to use with your own children?
- How varied were your own sources of information?
- Were you parents open, vague, judgmental, or absent in your education?
- What did you learn from your religion or spiritual tradition?
- Were there clear messages about morals, values, and acceptable behavior?
- Did the message vary between boys and girls?
- Where are the obvious holes in your education?
- What was the role of your culture?

You can see if other themes emerge. When parents are clear about their own upbringing and experiences they become better prepared to chart their own path of parenting rather than falling back on unconscious reactions. Using the list in the first part of the exercise, begin to write down what you want to tell your children from an informational standpoint. There are some items that get into values that are covered in the next chapter if you want to wait on them. Some of the items in the second exercise can be used to construct what you want your children to know as their parent, from your religion, or from your cultural heritage.

Here are some examples:

- Oral sex is when a person puts their mouth on the genitals of another person to give pleasure.
- Sexual coercion means that a person forces another to do sexual things without that person's consent. They may use threats, like not seeing them anymore or physcial threats. It is never okay to force someone to do something against their own desire or will.
- As your mother, I want you to know that sex is a powerful physical and emotional way to be close with another person. I would want you to know that sex has the power to be fantastic and just plain awful.
- If you ever have a scare about pregnancy or an STD, I hope you will come talk to me and let me help you. If you feel you can't, let's think of some safe people for you to go to.

Taking It All One Step Further

Some people hit the jackpot and their parents gave them

a thorough sex education and helped them learn what to expect in a healthy relationship. For everyone else, these exercises can point out holes in their learning and bring up painful memories. I've included an optional exercise that involves writing a letter to your parents, one that you never have to send, outlining what you wished they had told you about sex and relationships. When I suggest this, some people have an immediate negative reaction because of their relationship with their parents. They tell me they can't even imagine a best-case scenario. If that is you, simply think of an idealized parent or parents and do the exercise. We can't change our parents, but we can change our imagination and eventually, our own actions!

PURPOSE: To let go of memories and emotions that might get in your way and to show you the path you want to take with your own children.

HOW TO: Write a letter to your parents (both or separate) that says what you wished they had taught you about sex and about relationships. Let them know how important that would have been for you. Let your emotions and thoughts out about how you learned. Keep writing until you have said what you always wanted to say.

It is only in contemplation of our own personal experience that we can uncover our hidden assumptions, automatic reactions, and allay our own fears and concerns. Being able to fight off the automatic reactions to topics and questions is going to go a long way for parents to be able to most effectively communicate with their loved ones. When people think about what they missed in growing up they create a clearer path for their own parenting.

CHAPTER 5

Step 5:
Attuning Your Values

"To feel more fulfilled your actions and activities need to be in alignment with what you deem important."
— Deborah Day

All parents instill values in their children. In doing so, parents hope to positively affect their children's choices, attitudes, and behaviors, to teach them right from wrong, and to carry on certain traditions or customs. Some of how parents impart their values is purposeful, through discipline, nurturing, and education. However, children also learn values by observing how their parent's actions do or do not match their words.

It's not uncommon for people to choose their parenting partner based on a sense of shared values but when the children arrive discover they aren't on the same page. It's quite normal for this to happen in that none of us can imagine the scope of parenting until we are actually doing it. The exercises in Step 5 will take you through an exploration of your values to give you greater clarity about what they are and how to use them most effectively with your partner and children. It doesn't matter if you consider yourself liberal or conservative, religious or not, traditional or progressive. The goal here is simply to know yourself better.

Types of Values

All cultures share many of the same values, but it is personal choice that determines which values carry the greatest importance. Some examples include safety, respecting social norms, exploring, novelty, tradition, tolerance, and achievement. What people believe and value will also change across the lifespan as their focus moves from things like personal identity formation, education, and career development to creating a relationship or becoming a parent.

Values Clarification

Lacking a clear understanding of their values makes it more difficult for parents to be confident about answering their children's questions. Indeed, many parents have told me they actually *fear* questions their children might ask. It may be that parents lack sufficient knowledge about the question, but more often it is that parents haven't figured out how to translate their own values into meaningful, age-appropriate answers. They then avoid the topic altogether or lay down "the law" in a dictatorial way. These approaches rarely work with children who then simply go to other sources for their answers or rebel against what they perceive as meaningless rules. The result is that parents fail to transmit the very values they wanted their children to learn.

To be most successful in putting values into action, the experts tell us that the following steps are crucial. Values must be:

- chosen freely
- chosen among alternatives
- chosen after due reflection
- prized and cherished
- publicly affirmed
- acted upon, part of a pattern of repeated action

The exercises that follow will help you explore your most highly prized values and how to activate them in raising your children.

Exercise: Getting Clear On Values

For this exercise I have compiled a list of common values that pertain to relationships and to sexuality. Feel free to add any that have meaning for you.

PURPOSE: To identify specific values that you can put into action in your parenting.

HOW TO: Use the scale that follows to indicate the value you place on each item with regard to teaching your children about relationships and sexuality.

4 – of supreme importance to me
3 – very important to me
2 – important to me
0 – not important to me

Values List

____ 1. Honesty
____ 2. Fidelity
____ 3. Kindness
____ 4. Self-control
____ 5 Trustworthiness
____ 6. Respect
____ 7. Self-expression
____ 8. Responsible decision-making
____ 9. Right to pleasure
____ 10. Accurate Information
____ 11. Openness to experience

____ 12. Right to Consent
____ 13. Religious teachings/traditions
____ 14. Cultural norms/traditions
____ 15. Self-care (emotional, physical)
____ 16. Tolerance for differences
____ 17. Other____

Going back through the list, what of your top values relate to what you want your children to learn about being in relationships? What has most importance for you in teaching your children about sexuality? I expect there will be some overlap. Now, let's see how you want to apply them to what your children will learn from you.

Exercise: Putting Values into Action

After your due reflection, let's consider some specific topics that people learn about relationships and sexuality. This list is not exhaustive (40 seemed like a lot!), so feel free to add items of importance to you. The items on this list are also more broadly relevant to tweens and teens. However, young children do get information from any number of sources, so being clear now will help you brooch the topic at appropriate times and answer those tricky questions from your kids.

PURPOSE: To explore which values matter when considering certain topics about sex and relationships.

HOW TO: Using the list of values from the first exercise, go through this list and write down which values apply to each topic. More than one value could easily apply.

- Privacy for one's own body/sexuality
- Proper hygiene
- Good touch/bad touch talk
- Masturbation
- Pregnancy
- Gender roles
- How to be a good friend
- Use of birth control
- Coping with emotional changes/reactions from others
- Opposite sex attraction and behavior
- Dating behaviors (acceptable behavior on a date)
- Protection from STDs/STIs
- Intimate relationships
- Intercourse
- Oral sex, anal sex, or other mutual sexual behaviors
- Becoming sexually active/when sexual behavior is appropriate
- Same sex attraction and behavior
- Abortion
- Violence in relationships
- Sexual coercion
- Pornography

EXERCISE REMINDER

REFLECT ON YOUR VALUES
STAY IN THE MOMENT
ACCEPT WHERE YOU ARE TODAY

- Use of drugs/alcohol
- What characteristics to look for in a romantic partner
- Monogamy/fidelity in a relationship
- How to handle rejection
- How to break up with someone
- Prostitution/Sex Work
- Sexual harassment
- Rape
- Divorce
- Interfaith dating
- Living with someone before marriage
- Sexual fantasies
- Emotional intimacy
- Sexual fulfillment
- Taking advantage of someone who cannot give consent due to being altered or drunk or mentally incapable
- Nudity
- Respect
- The connection of sex to relationships
- Sexting

Putting It All Together

To conclude this exploration of your values, take highlighters or colored markers and highlight your list according to this guide (use all that apply):

Blue: I clearly know what my values are for this topic

Green: I am secure in my knowledge about this topic

Red: I am confused or conflicted about my values or knowledge of this topic

Now you have a better understanding of directions for your own preparation. If you are not clear on your values yet, a look back at your exercises in Step 4 may reveal certain road blocks or experiences that left you confused or conflicted. If you don't feel knowledgeable about certain topics you can find help in Steps to come.

CHAPTER 6

Step Six:

Teaming Up With Your Partner

"The goal in marriage is not to think alike, but to think together." —Robert C. Dodds

Conflicts about parenting styles, beliefs, values, even gender roles can cause great distress for couples. The major task of this Step, as you will see, is to consciously develop positive ways to express yourself that will, in turn, increase your openness and willingness to talk about difficult topics with your co-parent. Single parents don't despair—you can do the exercises as well and learn much more about yourself by teaming up with a trusted family member or friend. Through the exercises in this chapter all parents will learn how to be flexible, to better control the ways of expressing emotions, and fundamental skills for keeping families happy and connected.

Understanding Parenting Styles

Parenting styles are usually identified in three main positive categories: authoritarian, authoritative, and permissive. They represent a broad approach to parenting and represent specific parenting behaviors geared toward socializing a child; that is, how parents expect their children to behave in relation to other people. Let's look at each one separately.

Authoritarian Parenting

Having an authoritarian parenting style indicates that parents view their children as being in need of solid authority to curb their inherent strong will and tendency to be self-indulgent. Authoritarian parents think that having these qualities is the potential cause of unacceptable behavior, even, among the religiously minded in certain traditions, the root of sin. To avoid intolerable behavior, authoritarian parents believe they must bring the will of the child into line and that conscious obedience to a higher authority represents the path to happiness in life. They may have a lot of rules and explanations based on specific religious or cultural teachings, with little room for discussing them. Parents, when challenged, might be more likely to fall back on their authority alone, the "Because I say so" explanation. Authoritarian parents expect their children to fall quickly in line and to put aside their feelings and desires while accepting the parents' authority. For parents who value this style, this type of parental control over the child's self-will is the highest form of caring and an expression of their love.

Authoritative Parenting

Rather than rule by authority alone, authoritative parents value striking a balance between allowing for the child's expression of desires and offering explanations of their adult point of view. Thus, the parent reserves the right to set boundaries and rules while allowing some self-expression. Parents take the needs or desires of the child into account but do not indulge them at the expense of others. These parents expect their children to follow their lead and internalize cultural rules, which might be even more than authoritarian parents have. Consistency, rational discussion and emotional expression are hallmarks of this approach and exemplify the parents' love and caring.

Permissive Parenting

Both of the above approaches are assertive, that is, the parents are putting demands on the child to act within certain limits that the parents set. Permissive parenting, on the other hand, is described as non-demanding but with high parental involvement. Parents permit the child to freely express wants and desires and to act more impulsively, especially in relation to those desires. These parents see their role as guiding the child as they would a friend, with advice rather than rules. Discipline is rare and children are socialized to make their own decisions. Permissive parents view accepting and indulging the child's self-direction as nurturing and loving.

Outcomes of Parenting Styles

Not surprisingly, parenting styles affect children's behavior and sense of self in the world. Western culture research shows that an authoritarian parental approach results in children who are well-behaved on the surface, but who exhibit more emotional stress. They are also more apt to have deficit in social skills that make it more difficult for them to connect well with others.

An authoritative parental approach that includes both being responsive to the child as well as placing boundaries on behavior results in children who have fewer emotional problems, are more enterprising, and are socially skilled.

Finally, children of permissive parents feel loved, have good self-esteem, and fewer emotional difficulties. However, they are more likely to achieve less academically and to experiment with drugs and alcohol.

As most parents know, it's easy to find yourself saying and doing things your parents did that you promised yourself you would never to do to your own children. Rather than feeling guilty, or worse, shameful about that, now is the time to learn how to be clear about the parenting style you want to practice and to share that with your co-parent for collaboration and support.

For example, in my own upbringing with my two sisters, my father and mother initially leaned toward an authoritarian approach. When we were young, our parents punished our transgressions by spankings and disapproval, and we learned not to cross certain lines. Yet, as we grew up, our parents loosened the reins in terms of discussing opinions and desires. We had deep conversations and debates about the important issues of the times. Even so, if we didn't accept their point of view in the end, the authoritarian parts of their parenting came out full force. There were many incidences of yelling and dishes being swept from the table. I hated those interactions, as you might imagine, my father yelling his disapproval of my opinion and my mother simply shaking her head in disapproval of the method and content of my argument.

So, you can imagine my consternation when I became an adult and learned that I was considered formidable both in my roles as a parent and as a teacher. This really confounded me because I genuinely wanted to know my students' or children's thinking concerning what they did; I wanted us to debate and consider. What I learned is that my face looked so challenging in those moments that my loved ones and students sometimes didn't feel safe to express themselves.

Realizing how ingrained the lessons of both my parents had become, I had to work hard to physically change my facial expression and tone of voice. I had to ask my partner and children to tell me when I got "that look" on my face so I could take a deep breath and release the old patterns. I still explain to my students that when the look crosses my face it is about me thinking deeply and not about the quality of their words. Sometimes I jokingly tell them not to look at me when they make presentations. This shows how knowing the ways we might carry on dislikable family traditions allows us to create leverage with others for teaming up to make meaningful changes.

Attachment Style and Parenting

In Step 3 I introduced three main attachments styles: secure (low anxiety and avoidance), preoccupied (high anxiety and low avoidance), and avoidant (low anxiety and high avoidance). People respond, interact, and connect to others in their world based on their experiences with their own caretakers. Attachment style, developed from a person's own parental interactions, will affect that person's own parenting behaviors, as well as connection to a co-parent.

Preoccupied/Anxious Attachment and Parenting

People who have higher anxiety about their close relationships but are relatively lower in avoidance are classified in the preoccupied/anxious category. As a partner and parent, this person experiences negative self-talk, doubts about his or her skills, feels highly anxious as well as confused about how best to interact with others. In interpersonal relationships, the person comes across as wanting constant reassurance and connection, but not being able to accept it when offered.

In terms of co-parenting and communication, having a preoccupied/anxious attachment style can result in one of two approaches. Some parents attempt to minimize any differences in parenting style with the partner; others become overly involved with the children and completely exclude the other parent. Typically, anxiously attached people might gravitate toward a permissive parenting style in pursuit of the love and acceptance they crave.

Those who have preoccupied/anxious attachment have several different ways they strengthen their attachment, turning it into a more secure one. As I outlined in Step 2, one technique is to recognize and then consciously replace the negative or critical voices in your head. Also helpful is to develop reliable self-soothing or grounding skills that will help you be more comfortable having conversations with loved ones.

Avoidant Attachment and Parenting

Avoidant tendencies can vary from 'dismissive' to 'fearful,' depending on the amount of underlying anxiety the person has. Avoidantly attached people sometimes come across so independent they present themselves as not really needing connection or closeness. Their partners will generally describe them as tuned-out both as partners and parents. Yet, this simply isn't true. Avoidantly attached people have developed those strategies to numb the pain or avoid feeling rejected. They learned that showing emotions or being direct about desires were not the ways to achieve closeness; thus, they keep what they feel at a safe distance.

As parents, when their children are distressed about something, avoidantly attached people respond by allowing them to cry or fuss without comforting them. They believe that having their children "cry out" their distress, as they had to do themselves as children, will help them develop independence. Parents in this attachment style may not be particularly physically affectionate or willing to put aside their own interests to spend time with their children. Many of them find an authoritarian parenting style safer because a "Because I say so!" approach allows for more distance.

The tasks for avoidantly attached people are to develop skills that allows for more direct expressions of emotions and vulnerability as well as ways to reduce isolation and avoidance. It is easy to see how a charged subject like sex can be especially challenging for an avoidantly attached person.

Your Own Attachment and Parenting Styles

Becoming aware of your own attachment style will make it much easier to understand your thoughts and behavior. You will find many online questionnaires designed to help you further determine your personal attachment style. By sharing this information with your partner you can expand each other's sense of compassion and reduce the likelihood of taking the other's actions personally. The good news is that no one is stuck with an attachment style that is less than secure. This Step, which involves teaming up with your co-parent, provides the opportunity to shift your attachment style, to improve your communication skills, and to build greater satisfaction in your relationship.

You'll find that it is also helpful to identify the style your parents used when raising you, keeping in mind that they might have had two different styles. Using the following list of questions, review with your partner the parenting styles of both your parents' and yourselves.

- What do you value about what your parents did?
- Did their style change over time? Was it different based on gender? What do you wish to do differently from what your parents did?
- How can your partner best support your preferred parenting style?
- If there are differences in style, how will you use a team approach to honor your differences?

Understanding Your Relationship Communication Challenges

The basis of any successful relationship is being curious about a partner's point of view. Early in a relationship people usually spend a lot of time simply talking and listening as they learn about each other, thus creating extraordinary closeness and safety. This first stage of discovery and bonding is indeed magical, and it is also a crucial part of connecting as a couple. This process minimizes differences and maximizes similarities.

Yet, once settled into a daily routine, the talking, listening, and learning slows down. Differences become more apparent and people begin to speak more of their truth. They start to test the boundaries of their couple unit to see where there is room for their individual selves. World-renowned couples therapists, Ellyn Bader and Peter Pearson, explain that healthy relationships need to go through this process, known as differentiation. They define this stage as:

"The active, ongoing process of defining oneself and activating oneself in the context of a close interpersonal relationship and risking greater intimacy or separation."

Some people feel threatened about leaving the exclusive bonding phase to move into the phase of differentiation, perhaps fearful that their differences will reveal that they are ill-suited. To manage emerging differences they either try to avoid and withdraw from all conflict or fight and blame each other. To solidify a healthy relationship, partners must be willing to learn to speak their truth and actively listen to their partner's perspective. Communicating effectively about mundane aspects of life such as who will take out the trash or do the wash is crucial for tackling the deeper issues in relationships including parenting.

And Baby Makes Three

Bringing a child into a relationship is always going to

change the dynamics between the partners. Time spent together becomes limited, postpartum changes are often challenging, and whatever the couple's routine was (and however well it might have worked) is altered once child-rearing becomes part of it. The exclusive bonding time between parent and child may leave one partner feeling left out, time for sex and physical affection goes to the back burner, and strong differences about raising the child might emerge between the parents. According to research done by the Gottman Institute, 40% to 70% of couples admit that they contemplated divorce in the first three years after their baby was born.

Even among couples who have weathered the early stages of parenting and have formed a strong bond, preliminary attempts to discuss difficult topics may cause old patterns to resurface, be they of avoidance, withdrawal, or irritation and anger. If the subject at hand is teaching their child about sex, you can be sure that differences will emerge.

Fortunately, everyone can learn to communicate more effectively and about any topic. The exercises that follow describe techniques you can use to approach even delicate subjects with your partner and children.

Strategies for Successful Conversations

But first, a reminder: don't waste time beating yourself up about communication difficulties in the past. Simply acknowledge that they happened and that you are now learning ways to help you both avoid such difficulties. Here are some proven steps from experts that will lead you both to better communication strategies.

1. Ask your partner if he or she is willing to listen to what you have to say or to take part in these exercises.
2. Agree that you will focus on the topic raised or the specific exercise and will not let triggers take you off track to other topics in your relationship.
3. Speak about yourself and your own feelings and opinions rather than assuming you know what your partner thinks or feels.
4. If a topic or what you hear triggers either one of you, remind yourself that it's okay to take a break and that you do not own your partner's attitude or expectations.
5. If you do need a break, agree on how much time it will be and use that to self-soothe rather than arming yourself with arguments against your partner's point of view. Come back together in the agreed time and refocus on your goals including to learn more about yourself and your partner.
6. When your partner is sharing, put yourself fully in the listening mode. Cultivate an attitude of curiosity and ask questions for clarification. For example, say "Can you tell me more about why you feel uncomfortable using anatomically correct words for genitals?" rather than criticism such as, "Using pet names is stupid."
7. Stay away from blame, shame, or personal attacks

(e.g., "Your parents didn't have a clue about what they were doing when they taught you that!").

8. Accept that you are going to have differences of opinion and that right now you are not trying to solve anything. The focus here is to strengthen your bond as a couple and as parents by revealing more about yourself and learning more about your partner.
9. Finally, if things go off the rails, practice repair techniques to get back on track. Recognize if there is a need to reduce any flood of emotions that get in your way. Take responsibility for any reactions you have that are counterproductive (e. g., "Sorry, that item pushed me to a place that is tough for me--can we back up and let me try that again?"), or even acknowledge your appreciation for your partner's point of view.

Actively practicing these steps will help you learn to calmly and competently talk with your partner about your own attitudes, opinions, and values as well as learn about the other's world.

Learning More About Your Partner

A road to your partner's heart is exploring more about what makes this person unique. The first exercise in the following is to help you understand how your partner's parents and culture influenced his or her learning about sex and relationships. Following that are suggestions for sharing your sex and relationship lifelines [See Chapter 3] to expand your understanding of your partner's experience.

> **EXERCISE REMINDER**
>
> START WITH CURIOSITY
> LEARN ABOUT YOUR PARTNER
> CELEBRATE SIMILARITIES AND DIFFERENCES

Exercise: Discovering Your Partner's Past Influences

The focus of the question stems that follow is on what you and your partner learned growing up. After you share what you learned, feel free to talk about your beliefs now.

PURPOSE: To learn about and understand your partner's upbringing experiences.

HOW TO: Take turns answering the questions about how you perceive *your partner's experiences* with parents and culture. For example, with question #1, one of you would say to the other, "Your father thought sex … (was fun, a gift from God, etc.)." Your partner then takes a turn to answer that question about your father. Aim to spend about thirty minutes on this exercise. If you don't know the answer, take a guess and ask for the answer from your partner. Discovery and connection are your only goals.

- Your father thought that sex...
- The topic of masturbation for you....
- When you were growing up, your religion told you that sex...
- Your biggest fears about sex when you were young were....
- Your mother thought sex...

- When you were rejected by a person you were interested in, your (mother, father, etc.) told you to....
- In your culture, sex is thought of as....
- You learned that your body...
- For you, the topic of drugs and sex...
- If you tried to talk with your father about sex...
- If someone tried to hurt you emotionally, your parent(s)...
- When you were allowed to start dating, you were told...
- When you began dating someone, you were taught that sex should happen....
- Your father told you that a man...
- Your parent(s) taught you that violence within a relationship was....
- If you asked your mother about sex she...
- Your parent(s) taught you that love...
- Your mother told you that a woman....
- When in a relationship, your parents said being faithful was....
- You were taught that affection...
- If you ever had a scare about pregnancy or STDs, you talked with...
- When it comes to using protection against pregnancy or STDs, your parents said....
- Your mother said a man...

- You learned that girls who were sexually active were thought of as...
- Virginity....
- Your parent(s) taught you that homosexuality...
- For you, sex within a relationship is...
- In your family, you never talked about sex because...
- The person you went to if you had a question about sex was...
- Somebody who got an STD or got pregnant was thought of as...
- Your father said a woman was...
- The parent that gave you "the talk" was....
- If your parents disagreed about your upbringing they resolved it by....
- For your family, divorce...
- Your greatest fears about talking to our children about sex are...

At this point, consider sharing your sex and relationship lifelines with your partner as a way of furthering knowledge about each other. However, yours may contain memories you are not prepared or wish to share at this time. I firmly believe in respecting a partner's desire for privacy in this matter without suspicion or prying. If you do decide to share the results of your lifeline exercises, please consider the following instructions:

- The goal is to understand each other's experiences better.
- The knowledge you gain is for building your parenting team; that is, what lessons you have learned or how do you now understand how your and your partner's past might be shaping your approach to parenting?
- Without asking any questions initially, read through the lifeline keeping in mind your partner's perspective.
- Decide between the two of you any ground rules for discussing the lifelines.
- Strive to be aware of any triggers for yourself that you will need to manage and use self-soothing and grounding when necessary to stay present.
- Promise yourself and your partner that this knowl edge will be used in positive ways only.
- Alternatively, rather than sharing your actual chart, you may prefer simply to share impressions of your life story with respect to sexuality and relationships. For this address aspects such as:
- What are my most negative and positive experiences?
- Have I seen personal growth over time in my attitudes and beliefs?
- Which experiences do I think are particularly important as we prepare ourselves to teach our children about sex and relationships?
- What do I want my partner to understand most about me from these exercises?

Exploring Your Values and Approaches Together

The exercises in this next section are to help parents learn more about their partner's values. *There is no right or wrong here.* Couples agree and disagree on any number of areas of their lives such as how to handle finances, careers, housework, family and friends. Naturally you should expect to have some differences in values and opinions concerning how to teach your child about sex and relationships. Exploring your values and opinions together will help you create a stronger team approach.

Heterosexual couples might see some gender role expectation sneak in here. Research has clearly shown that mothers do most of the sex and relationship education. This fact may signal women that they should make more room for their male partner as a co-parent; indeed, women are not necessarily the more capable parent simply by virtue of their gender. Men in heterosexual relationships must always be mindful about this potential trap as well. Abdicating responsibility whether to avoid it or to keep the peace is likely to create some resentment in their partner.

Exercise: Sharing Values with Your Partner

PURPOSE: To explore each person's specific values in teaching children about sex and relationships

HOW TO: Taking turns, each person openly and honestly shares the top five values from the Getting Clear on Values Exercise in Step 5 that are most important to them. A short statement about why each value is important to you is helpful. The role of the listening partner is to focus on getting to know your partner better by reflecting back what you heard and asking for clarification.

Exercise: Values Action Plan

PURPOSE: To know your partner better. To create a shared values action plan for the sex and relationship education for your children.

HOW TO: Exchange personal lists from Step 5 with your partner to find areas where your values align and areas where you differ. With this in mind, discuss the areas where you feel secure in your knowledge as well as those for which you would like more information. Next, identify areas about which either one of you feels conflicted or confused.

Let's look at an example using proper hygiene for children. No doubt it is important for both of you, but the challenge is to teach your children about hygiene and, at the same time, remain supportive of each other. For example, with young kids, is it the end of the world if they miss a bath? Rather than have an ironclad rule, i.e. children must have a bath every night, focus instead on being able to accept influence from each other.

When it comes to areas in which you are not in full agreement, review and discuss them one by one. Some of the things on the list may not be relevant yet due to the age of your children. For example, the age when parents think a child can date may be a source of conflict, but if your child is five, there is no need to debate it now. Instead, use this exercise as an opportunity to explore and consider ideas and opinions rather than make a rule in advance. Revisit this list each year as your children continue to grow (and as you do as a parent!); reexamine your values and discuss how to put them into action.

When Parenting Values or Approaches Differ

Following are suggestions for how to compromise and complement your differences in values, as well attachment and parenting styles. Doing so will enable you to more confidently parent your children.

- If you have differences in attachment styles, be aware and respectful of tendencies toward avoidance or anxiety in yourself and your partner.
- If there is an area of parenting that brings up a lot of anxiety in one person, check to see if the partner might be willing to tackle it alone or be willing to do it as a team. Accept differences and model cooperation.
- If your parenting styles differ, ask your partner to explain the reasoning behind a decision and listen fully. Get below the surface to see if childhood experiences are pushing certain positions.
- If culture or religion are part of your parenting decisions, openly discuss not only the rationale but also how to manage differences so one on you is is not undermining the other.
- As much as possible, discuss parenting differences away from your children. Undermining the other

parent in front of the kids will easily kill a relationship.

- When your children are older, family meetings are a good way for all parties to be heard and considered. Children might well have solutions their parents haven't thought of. Furthermore, these conversations encourage positive problem-solving.

This chapter covered a lot of ground about steps to help you form a strong co-parenting team (or in the case of single parents, to enlist the support of loved ones). Accomplishing this goal will require many conversations to fully explore the many topics you will need to consider. Should you find you are having trouble maintaining your agreement to disagree or compromise, discussing this with a parenting coach or therapist, or attending parenting workshops together can be a great help. Although my own children are now adults, I still find there are parenting challenges about sex and relationships. I have learned to strive for continued progress and to release the goal of perfection from myself as a partner or parent.

CHAPTER 7

Step 7:
Getting the Facts

"Comments are free, but facts are sacred."
—C.P. Scott

Part of the preparation for important conversations with your children is getting the facts, in particular, which ones are age-appropriate to discuss. In this Step I provide a topic outline for you that is in sync with your children's maturation. You'll also find information about how to address topics at a deeper level in accordance with your children's progression from childhood to adolescence through young adulthood. Additionally, there is a variety of resources that are helpful for educating children about sex and relationship.

Age Appropriate Topics for Sex and Relationship Education

The following is a somewhat exhaustive list of topics to cover with your children as they grow up. Some of them are easy while others are more challenging and possibly even a bit scary for you to consider. In addition to learning from you, children will get information about many of these topics through their own development and interactions with family, friends, school, and media. Life presents lots of what are known as teachable moments, and the follow-up questions your kids might ask you will present many.

Infancy (birth-3) – names for genitals, gender differences, positive touch, trust, and how to comfort themselves

Early Childhood (4-5) – basic reproduction, their own bodies, privacy, masturbation, consent, private vs. public behaviors, body image, gender identity, communication skills, societal gender roles and expectations, and gender diversity

Middle Childhood (6-8) – sexual orientation, sexuality in relationships, more on privacy, respect, friendships, bullying or picking on others, nudity, how their bodies are changing and hints of puberty, more about human reproduction, perhaps intercourse, consent again, okay to be modest, expressing feelings, sense of self, and communication skills

Tweens (9-12) – puberty (menstruation, nocturnal emissions or wet dreams), emotional changes, emotional attachments, Internet and cyber boundaries (porn, violence), depictions of sex and relationships in media, positive aspects of sexual intimacy, risks, basics of contraception, process of birth, body changes and image, more on hygiene, physical exams related to reproduction (pelvic exam, testicular check, prostate exam), HPV vaccines, desire and sexual feelings, fantasy, peer pressure, healthy relationships, crushes and intense infatuations with people and things, different ways people express themselves sexually (manual, oral, anal, vaginal), more on sexual orientation, the value of abstinence, friendships, refusal skills, effects of drugs and alcohol on decision-making, managing rejection, gender respect, transgender phenomenon, the process of transitioning and gender-bending, sexting and cell phone use, sexual harassment, masturbation, and honoring promises made to another (fidelity), honesty, spirituality and sexuality

Teenagers (13-18)– continued physical and emotional changes (including identity), dating and relationships, more info on contraception and protection, responsibility, more on consent, more on how people express themselves sexually, sexual orientation, how sexual and emotional feelings interact, independence and responsibility, more on consent and sexual violence, decision-making, love, healthy relationship skills, sexual aids and toys, more on managing rejection, prevention of emotional and physical problems, more on gender respect, having a baby as a teen (including legal obligations), alternative sexual lives, prostitution or sex work, age of consent laws in your state or country, honesty, monogamy or fidelity, polyamory, ending a relationship honorably, more details of medical checkups including preparing for assessment of genitals and pelvic exam, breast self-exam, reproductive health, sexual problems and dysfunctions, more on masturbation and its role in healthy sexuality, more on the process of gender transition, more on the role of fantasy in sexuality, what to do if their sexual desires are inappropriate or illegal, cheating, and building trust in relationships

Young Adulthood (18-35) – more on dating and more on consent, entering into more lasting romantic relationships or marriage, sexual orientation, healthy relationship skills, boundaries (emotional and physical), emotional self-soothing while navigating the dating scene, more on sexual dysfunctions or problems, financial aspects of relationships and protecting one's assets, spotting signs of power and control by a partner (the cycle of violence) as well as ways to get out if caught up in an unhealthy relationship, sexual and reproductive health including checkups and using protection and birth control, kink and sexual minorities, self sexuality and shared sexuality as part of their lifetime experience, continuing the conversation about acting on sexual or compulsive desires that might harm others or are illegal

As An Example...

For an example of how a common discussion topic changes as children grow, let's look at hygiene. As toddlers, children are ready for potty-training and with it parents take certain steps to teach them preliminary information about hygiene. Once kids have become pretty reliable about signaling their need to go, parents can teach them how to clean their genitals and anus after they are finished. Even in these early phases, parents can explain certain basic facts to them, including how to pull back the foreskin to pee, and, for girls, how to wipe from front to back, plus how to be sure they are clean after pooping. Do they understand everything parents are saying right away? Probably not, as there are many steps to learn. At this time parents also explain why washing hands is important after using the toilet ("You could spread germs or get sick"). Do they know what a germ is? Again, probably not. This may not matter so much to kids, but they can tell it matters to their parent.

Now, let's consider how, as children are entering into puberty, the discussion of hygiene takes on different components. By now kids have a more sophisticated understanding of, for example, what germs are and that people can get infections like the common cold from one another. In these years hygiene education includes how puberty will change their bodies, growing hair in different places where it wasn't before – their armpits, around their genitals (vulva and base of the penis) and anus, on their legs and maybe their face. Hormone levels in their body create many of these changes, causing them to perspire more, smell different, get pimples or acne, start their periods, and experience wet dreams (nocturnal emissions). These changes offer parents the opportunity to provide more information about the importance of hygiene and why properly done helps reduce the possibility of infection.

What really changes about how parents talk to a three-year-old vs. a child of 12 is the amount of detail. Frankly, with more detail generally comes more discomfort. It is easy to explain certain things to very young children, but not so much as kids age. But they continue to need accurate and positively delivered information. I remember my own mother's not-so-kind lesson about hygiene when I reached puberty. She told me I needed to bathe more often and when I asked why, she answered, "You smell!" Not too much positive there in a response that made me feel extremely self-conscious about how my body smelled to others. Just to clarify, I don't blame my mother for this because I am aware that her parents gave her no sex education. But imagine how delivering information in a gentle and supportive way about body changes in puberty can help children feel positive toward their body image and self-esteem.

Exercise: Developing Your Sex Education List

It is now time for you to identify what information you need for your own sex and relationship education. This exercise as well as the suggestions that follow will help you get started.

PURPOSE: To identify what topics you need more information about; to deepen an understanding of your values about these topics, and to identify any emotional reactions that block your progress.

HOW TO: Going through the previous list of age-appropriate discussion topics, write down any areas you think you need to know more about, areas where expanding your knowledge of the topic will help you better explain it. In another column, write down the topics where you need a deeper exploration of your values and beliefs. In a third column list the topics that trigger emotional responses in you and create roadblocks.

ACTION STEPS: Review each topic one at a time to decide how you will move forward. How will you learn more about it? How will you consider your values in relationship to the topic? What self-soothing techniques or ways to get more specific help might be useful to you? Finally, single out topics that you feel you just cannot talk directly about with your child. It is important to honor yourself. Mobilize your support team and sound out your partner, family, and close friends (or even trusted professionals such as a religious leaders, social workers, therapists, peer educators, etc.) to see what help you can get.

Resources

There are many excellent sources of information that are available to parents. Here I have compiled some of the best examples for you to choose from and have included, where I can, a description of what the resource offers. I encourage all parents to search for resources themselves that match their own cultural, moral, and spiritual beliefs plus examples of books, organizations, and websites where you can learn more about these topics.

Books

Young children

Krasny, Laurie (2000). *What's the big secret? Talking about sex with girls and boys.* Little, Brown Books for Young Readers. An excellent book for children about 4 years and up that can help parents start the conversations they want to have. With lots of questions that cover the basics, parents and children can read this book together.

Mayle, Peter (2000). *Where did I come from? A guide for children and parents.* Penguin Random House Publisher Services. Suitable for children 5 and up, this book is a standard in the field. With age-appropriate illustrations, there are great examples of ways to explain the facts of life.

Saltz, Gail (2008). *Amazing you!: Getting smart about your private parts.* Puffin Books. Appropriate for the preschool crowd with cartoons to help educate kids about parts of their body. It is straightforward without being as detailed as other books in this category

Tweens and Teens

Cole, J. (2009). *Asking About Sex and Growing Up: A Question-and-Answer Book for Kids.* HarperCollins Publishers LLC. With a focus on tweens, information is presented in a question-and-answer format to provide straightforward information on a wide variety of subjects related to sex and puberty.

Harris, Robie (2014). *It's Perfectly Normal: Changing Bodies, Growing Up, Sex and Sexual Health*. Candlewick. Another standard in the field that has been recently updated. It is appropriate for mid- to older teens as the information is given in detail and there are cartoon illustrations that are realistic in their depictions.

Mayle, P. (2000). *What's Happening to Me? A Guide to Puberty*. Lyle Stuart, Inc. Designed to ease the embarrassment of explaining puberty to children, this book presents the facts of life during puberty. It aims to present the facts with honesty, sympathy and a sense of humor.

Madaras, L. (2007) *What's Happening to My Body? Book for Boys*. William Morrow Paperbacks. Updated and geared for tweens and teens. Madaras covers not only the physical changes associated with puberty, but includes important topics like emotions, romance, respect, and communication. Both books in the series contain a section on puberty for the opposite sex.

Madaras, L. (2007) *What's Happening to My Body? Book for Girls*. William Morrow Paperbacks. Updated and geared for tweens and teens. As with her book for boys, she covers not only the physical changes associated with puberty, but includes important topics like emotions, romance, respect, and communication. Both books in the series contain a section on puberty for the opposite sex.

Schwartz, P & Cappello, D. (2000). *Ten Talks Parents*

Must Have with Their Children About Sex and Character. Hyperion Books. Based on parenting workshops with proven success, the 'ten talks' approach can help give parents more specific ideas when they to talk with your children about sex, relationships, and character.

Young Adults

Joannides, P. & Gröss, D. (2015). *Guide to Getting it On.* 8th ed. Goofy Foot Press. I have used this book for undergraduate and graduate sex education and it is one of the best books around for any adult.

Organizations and Websites

Advocates for Youth
http://www.advocatesforyouth.org
A comprehensive website for parents and youth, this has a great deal of accurate and empowering information about reproductive and sexual health. There are specific areas about different types of sex education, parent-child communication, violence and harassment, religion and spirituality to name a few. In various sections below I reference specific pages from this website.

Sexuality Information and Education Council of the United States
www.siecus.org

With a mission to make accurate and comprehensive sex education available to all, this organization provides a great deal of information for anyone seeking to learn more. In addition, articles on a variety of topics including parent-child communication about sexuality. It also lists resources for faith-based communities.

Planned Parenthood

http://www.plannedparenthood.org/parents/talking-to-kids-about-sex-and-sexuality

This section of the Planned Parenthood website provides a wealth of tools including videos and dialogue examples that make the material easier to grasp and process. The website is beneficial to all parents seeking to educate their children and promote healthy sexuality and healthy communications. A variety of FAQs allow parents to focus on their important questions, such as how to start talking about sexuality with kids and how early such education should begin. There are a variety of other resources such as parenting teens who may be sexually active or helping teens delay having sex.

Talk With Your Kids

http://www.talkwithyourkids.org/pages/parents.htm

This site from the California Family Health Council is a good example of what various states are offering their residents. It gives examples of how parents can build trust, provide support, and share their values with their children. There is also information on teens' healthcare rights.

Parents and Friends of Lesbians and Gays (PFLAG)
http://community.pflag.org/Page.aspx?pid=194&srcid=-2
http://www.pflagatl.org/2013/05/when-you-think-your-son-or-daughter-is-gay/
The first link above is to the national organization, one of the oldest organizations to support parents, families, friends, and allies of LGBTQ (lesbian, gay, bisexual, trans, and queer) people. The second link is an excellent example from PFLAG Atlanta of what parents of a child they think is gay might consider, say, and do.

Religious Resources and Curricula

Advocates for Youth – Communities of Faith
http://www.advocatesforyouth.org/serced/2045-selected-sexuality-education-resources-for-communities-of-faith
This site offers information on selected resources from many religions: Catholic, United Methodist, Orthodox Church in America, Church of the Brethren and Mennonite, Evangelical Lutheran, Non-denominational Christian, Jewish, Episcopalian, and Unitarian Universalist groups. Curricula cover different age groups with some geared toward adults. Other topics of focus are on GBLT

communities or courses for parents.

Focus on the Family

www.focusonthefamily.com/parenting/sexuality

This faith-based website is designed to help parents talk to their children about many aspects of sex and relationships. The website aims to help parents feel more comfortable about talking to their children about sex and sexuality, and how to incorporate their faith into teaching about them. It suggests certain books and bible passages to read to relieve uneasiness, useful for those having a difficult time navigating how to teach their kids about sex while being true to their beliefs and faith.

Religious Institute

www.religiousinstitute.org

This is a multi-faith organization with the mission to promote sexual health, education, and justice not only in our society, but within faith communities as well. There are more than seven faith traditions represented in its national network.

Dating, Consent, and Domestic Violence

Love is Respect

http://www.loveisrespect.org

With an outreach geared toward teens regarding dating and relationship boundaries, this is an excellent resource for parents when they talk with their children about these topics. The website also offers direct support connections through a peer hotline, text, or by chat.

Family Life

http://www.familylife.com/articles/topics/parenting/ages-and-stages/teens/establishing-dating-guidelines-for-your-teen

This Christian website has many resources that parents may find helpful. It features an example of a parent talking with his teen daughter about physical lines she might cross with her date and examples to help parents establish dating guidelines, cell phone use, and Internet communication.

WebMD

http://www.webmd.com/parenting/features/teen-dating-guide-for-mom

This site has information that may surprise parents who think that they know what their children are doing when they are not looking. It has many facts about kids' social and sexual lives including what kids think of oral sex, when they are more likely to be sexually active (the afternoon!), girls asking out boys, and kids' online activity.

For parents of gender variant children

This is a fairly new area in parenting and the resources and advice vary tremendously from site to site. The ones I've chosen here have content from science-based sources.

Human Rights Campaign

http://www.hrc.org

This organization promotes human rights for lesbian, gay, bisexual, and transgender people. It features links for parenting, religion and faith, coming out, children and youth, hate crimes against LGBT individuals, and partnering with schools to support children and youth, just to name a few.

The Impact Program

http://www.impactprogram.org/families-blog/resources-for-parents-of-gender-variant-children/#sthash.HNI0GNkS.dpbs

This website contains webinars, blogs, research, and other resources for LGBTQ youth and for families. The link here is specifically for parents of gender-variant children.

Shepherd Express

http://shepherdexpress.com/article-21373-sexpress-resources-for-parents-of-gender-variant-children.html

One of the best resources to learn more about what being LGBTQ means; it features recently published books, community organizations, blogs, events, and other information sources for trans youth and their families.

For parents of children with emotional, physical, or intellectual disabilities

Here are resources for parents of a child or adult child with emotional, physical or intellectual disabilities. (I provide much more information in Chapter 11.)

Advocates for Youth

http://www.advocatesforyouth.org/publications/publications-a-z/479-sex-education-for-physically-emotionally-and-mentally-challenged-youth

Once again, AFY is the go-to website for information. This page has a discussion regarding the number of youth with disabilities, myths and facts about sexuality and disability, important parent guidelines, and selected resources.

Autism Sex Education

http://www.autismsexeducation.com/#!books/c491

All about autism and other developmental disabilities, this website is a thorough guide to sex education, social skills, training, methods for reaching children with neuro-atypical brains, parenting tips, and resources for your children.

Center for Parent Information and Resources

http://www.parentcenterhub.org/repository/sexed/

This site has a variety of sex education resources for children with various types of disabilities. It provides information on dating and disabilities and how a particular disability might affect a person's sexuality. Specific sex education curricula are referenced for those who want to know how to deliver quality sex education.

Sexual Minorities

Not surprisingly, there isn't a lot out there for parents when it comes to talking about what is meant by BDSM, kink, or being a sexual minority. I'm betting this is an area that most parents don't know much about or would be comfortable with, but I'm also betting that most teens have heard about *Fifty Shades of Grey*. The resources I've listed here discuss consensual adult behavior that sex researchers do not consider to be mental illnesses, but that represent the wide variety of ways adults seek consensual pleasure and relationships.

Agnostic Zetetic

https://agnosticzetetic.wordpress.com/2013/03/18/bdsm-and-children/

An enlightening blog about how one who is involved in kink (BDSM) could talk with their children in an age appropriate way about what constitutes kinky behavior.

In the end it is about how a parent is describing adult sexual/affectional behavior in a kink-positive way.

Modern Explanation of kinky vs. paraphilias
http://www.thefrisky.com/2013-01-18/fetishes-101-all-the-basics-about-having-a-sexual-fetish-or-paraphilia/
It isn't easy to understand the differences between what professionals in the mental health field would call a paraphilia (that is, something impulsive and compulsive that might be done without the consent of another person) and the variation in adult consensual sexual and emotional behavior. Parents can learn more about what someone who is in a sexual minority thinks about it all.

Illegal Sexual Behavior

ParentMap
https://www.parentmap.com/article/talking-to-kids-about-rape
This provides excellent information about rape. It gives facts about it and advice on how to start when your children are young to help them understand what consent and what rape actually mean. Parents are often surprised to learn that about 87% of sexual assaults are by people known to the victim (acquaintances or intimate partners), and that drugs/alcohol are often involved.

Virtuous Pedophiles

http://www.virped.org

This is admittedly a very difficult topic in our society in general. However, I bring the issue about people who are attracted to minors into the mix to help parents learn more about it and perhaps reach a child who has this attraction. This group and website is to educate the general public about people attracted to minors but who do not want to act on it. By reducing stigma, the developers believe that they can help pedophiles make the responsible choice not to act on their attractions and to lead healthy and happy lives. The site includes FAQs, resources, research, and ways to get help.

CHAPTER 8

Step 8:
The Talk: How You Show Up

"May what I do flow from me like a river, no forcing and no holding back, the way it is with children."
— Rainer Maria Rilke

Are you still feeling a bit nervous about actually talking with your child? Then you are pretty normal. To help ease you into it, in this Step you will be learning two major skills. First is how to initiate these talks by choosing naturally occurring times to open up conversations. Second, while people believe that what they say is the most important part of communication, what you convey with your tone of voice, facial expressions, and body posture is just as vital. I will show how you how to discover your personal nonverbal styles and how to make yourself more approachable and open.

Choosing Optimal Times for Talks

If your child or children are young, you have a head start

in making conversations about sex and relationships seem pretty normal to them. You also can demonstrate that you are a parent they can comfortably come to with questions. If, on the other hand, your children are approaching puberty, you are likely to meet with resistance and awkwardness. Those of you who are starting to change your parenting or attachment style should also expect your children to offer some initial resistance. Change is hard for everyone, so don't be surprised if at first you are faced with some sullenness, embarrassment, anger, or even outright refusal to accommodate the changes you are making.

Consequently, the best ways to introduce change depend somewhat on the age of your children. If they are, say, four or older but not yet nine or ten, taking a subtle approach can be helpful. Focus on gradually changing things and slip in your new direction at appropriate times. For example, if you haven't talked about where babies come from or hotter topics such as masturbation, try bringing home books on a number of different topics, including those. Tell your reading-age child or children that you found some things in the books that you thought might interest them. Then leave the books with them to sort through on their own.

As a follow-up on this, avoid posing a direct question, such as, "What did you think of the book on how babies are made?" A more subtle approach would be to throw out a comment like, "I really liked the pictures in that book." Or, "Which book was your favorite?" Now, if the children seem to be open to talking about what they saw in the books, you can try a less subtle approach such as, "I sure wish I had a book like this when I was growing up. My parents didn't think it was proper to talk about our private parts."

It's best if you say only a little at a time and leave lots of room for your child's responses. If you find yourself babbling on or pressing your child with words or body language (more about this later in this Step), take a deep breath and practice some silent self-soothing. Some children may be more comfortable writing down questions and having their parents give them a written or verbal answer. It's about being inventive and sensitive to your personality and that of your child. The goal is starting the topic and being clear that you are open to having these kinds of conversations.

If your child doesn't respond right away, your job is to smile reassuringly, stay low key, and wait for the next opportunity. Disappointment, frustration, anger, or pressing for a discussion will not work. Change really does take time and it's only through practice and persistence that habits change. Stay with your commitment to make time for conversations, whether you initiate them or your child is the one asking the questions. I will help you create an action plan later in this chapter.

Team Building

You don't have to do this alone. I am hopeful that you and your co-parent (or a close relative or friend) have completed the exercises in Step 5 and have some agreement about how you will work together. Creating a tag team helps your child see that the two of you are in this parenting thing together and that you are both approachable for questions and comments. After reading this book you are still not sure you can be the point person for certain questions about sexuality or relationships, it's vital to designate another adult or adults to be your child's source(s) of information. This takes the burden off any one individual. Single parents, search out family members or trusted friends who can support you and be another adult available to your child to talk with. It's important to know that you don't have to do this part of parenting alone.

Opening Up Conversations

Parents of an older child may decide it's time to have that 'talk,' but confront resistance, embarrassment, and disgust at their attempts. A more subtle approach as I described previously is fine if it fits your or your child's style. But you might simply ask to meet with your child and your co-parent and be direct. For example, "I bet you are wondering why we asked to have a talk with you. We (I) actually need to come clean about something we've (I've) been having some trouble with... (talking with you about sex, sexuality, and relationships). We've (I've) been uncomfortable to say much because... (my parents didn't talk with me, I wasn't sure what age to start, we (I) felt embarrassed). We (I) want to start being more open and available to talk with you and answer your questions."

The first part of your job is to show your children that you are dedicated to changing the way you communicate with them. Explain that you have learned most kids want their parents to talk with them about sex and relationships. Tell them as well that you've learned that kids whose parents teach them the facts and their values make healthier decisions about love and sex. Share how much you want them to be both safe and happy. These statements show that you are putting value on these conversations.

The second part is to take responsibility and be humble about the fact you haven't been very effective in teaching them about healthy sex and relationships thus far. You can mention briefly that most people don't get much education from their parents and you've come to realize that isn't the way you want to be. You are now modeling something important for your children; you are not perfect and you are willing to change yourself to be a better parent.

The third part is to open up the conversation by asking them how they think your family communication can be improved. Commit to having a family meeting once a month for at least six months; being consistent and participating actively in the meetings and your conversations will likely overcome initial resistance to change, lack of participation, and bad attitudes.

What is Guaranteed to Fail

What is sure to shut down communication is to ask your child what he or she knows about sex. I know some people suggest this (and I've seen it on parenting websites), but imagine if someone asked you that question. Given that the word 'sex' is used to convey a substantial variety of aspects of human sexuality, it's easy to see that a child may feel overwhelmed by the question and will likely feel put on the spot. The rationale behind this approach is no doubt that the parent could just fill in or correct the information, but as we know the topics of sexuality and relationships are multilayered and it's impossible to cover everything in one talk.

Understanding your current style of talking and listening is key to making changes in your parent-child communication, just as it is in talking with your partner or another adult. Do you create an atmosphere in which your loved ones feel safe bringing up certain topics? Or does your approach invite them to lie? Most parents would say they don't want their children to lie, but parents can give the impression that they can't handle the truth and it isn't safe to tell the truth. The implication might be that truth-telling will result in a punishment or an otherwise harsh reaction.

For example, when I was about 13 years old I liked to hang out with some of my friends after school. The girls and boys would occasionally kiss or make out a bit, but nothing heavy. I don't know if my father heard about this from another parent or if he was just thinking I was about the right age to be interested in kissing, but when I came home one day he asked me to tell him what we were doing after school. I said that we had been goofing around a little and kissing. Instead of continuing the conversation and supporting me in telling the truth, he decided I was lying. In response, he started to shout at me and accuse me of doing much more, staring intently at me and standing over me as he made his accusations.

What, then did this teach me? To lie and to tell him nothing that was really going on, to play the innocent. This is how parents end up getting get the opposite of what they say they want from their children. My father didn't make it safe for me to tell the truth. Sadly for both of us our relationship, which had been pretty close and trusting to that point, started to fracture, especially around my growing up and going into puberty.

The Role of Nonverbal Behavior

As you may have noticed from my story, it wasn't just what my father was saying that broke some of my trust, it was also how he said it. Children look at their parents' faces from day one and rely mostly on nonverbal behavior (nonverbals), such as facial expressions and tone of voice, to decode their world.

Children build trust between themselves and their parents by observing how much match-up there is between parental nonverbal and verbal behaviors. They easily pick up on any inconsistencies between facial expressions, tone of voice, and other nonverbals, and actual words. Some experts in the field of communications refer to this incongruence as "false acceptance." These inconsistencies may be tied to your parenting style (being more permissive) or your attachment style (wanting acceptance, thus refusing to say no or what you want for fear of rejection). The danger is creating an environment in which the child develops less-than-secure attachment because parental words and actions don't match up. Children begin to believe that the world isn't safe, that parents and others really can't be trusted, and, possibly, that they can't trust their own choices.

Understanding Nonverbals

In interactions with other people, nonverbal behavior conveys about 60% of a person's underlying meaning. Not surprisingly, that percentage is higher with very young children as they don't understand much of what is said to them and so underlying meaning comes primarily from nonverbals. Children also learn to interpret emotions through others' nonverbal behavior. They easily learn how to gauge the mood or approachability of their parents and others, as well as gauging the safety to interact (both emotionally and physically).

Such things as body position, facial expression, and even at times, breathing patterns strongly convey how humans communicate their willingness to connect with others. We learn nonverbals through interaction with family, our culture, and feedback from others and almost unconsciously use verbal and nonverbal cues in conversations. This includes how we open a conversation, who gets to speak first, eye contact, interrupting rules, nodding, laughing, gestures, etc. Nonverbals can be clear without language (putting a finger to your lips to denote silence) and can assist our words (nodding your head as you say you agree). They can indicate our emotional state (shoulders slumped and head down when feeling sad), regulate our interactions with others (looking away when someone approaches to show you do not wish to interact), or help us adapt to or manage a situation (crossing our arms over our torso when we feel challenged). Nonverbals can also be used to hide what we feel or think (shutting down all facial expressions or putting on a happy face when we don't feel it).

Even the sounds we make and our speech patterns serve as important cues. Some of these patterns are inborn. For example, men's voices are usually lower and may project farther than women's voices. Voice volume is important as it may be scary or threatening to children, even when there is no threat meant. Speech patterns of how we describe our world come from our experience. A vivid example is the role culture plays in how animal sounds are described. In English we describe a pig's grunt as oink oink, while in Dutch it is knor knor, and in Japanese it is boo boo. Tone of voice is crucial in conveying meaning – think about saying "I love you" in a normal tone of voice versus a whisper, yelling it, saying it quickly or very slowly, or angrily. Speaking loudly is normal in some cultures and considered rude in others.

All this points out the need to be aware of these vocal speech patterns and how they affect loved ones. The following exercises will help you decode your own nonverbals and change those that get in the way of open communication.

Exercise: Decoding Your Nonverbal Behaviors

There are two parts to this exercise. In part one, you explore your nonverbal communication on your own to increase your awareness of how others experience you. You will learn what you do and how well this is working for you.

◆ PART 1

PURPOSE: To become personally aware of your nonverbals.
HOW TO: For one day focus your awareness on your nonverbal behavior when you are with your child or children (or other people in your life). Using the list generated below, note your behaviors:

Body language

- Eye contact (direct vs. indirect), looking at them or away while listening
- Stance (hands on hips, shoulders hunched, back turned)

- Gestures (hand out to stop, thumbs up, nodding, wringing your hands, making a fist)
- Facial expression, (scowling, smiling, mirroring your child's expression, looking stern)
- Posture (relaxed, open, guarded)
- Movement (walking, quick movements, pacing, waving hands or arms)
- Physical contact (hugging, touching gently, grabbing part of body to direct attention, avoidance of physical contact)

Tone of voice and voice elements

- Flat (always maintaining the same tone, no emotion)
- High (depending on the age of the child)
- When conveying negative emotions such as disappointment, anger, frustration (tsking, raised voice, frequently repeating yourself)

Use of interpersonal space

- Distance from the child or person
- How close you get (does this change with the message?)
- Getting on the child's level
- Getting busy doing something else in the room while you are talking to the person

Objects

- Do your clothes communicate something about your

availability and attention?

Time

- How much time are you able to spend with your child or children?
- Are you mainly paying attention to what they are doing wrong and not what they are doing right?

Assess Yourself

What do you notice about your nonverbal behaviors from the list above? Use these questions to learn more and add any that are important to you.

- Do you avoid eye contact so you don't have to be aware of the reaction of your child?
- What is the reaction of your loved ones to your facial expressions?
- Is your tone of voice always the same?
- Do your nonverbals vary based on the time of day or when your co-parent or other people are around?
- Do your nonverbals match your verbal statements or your emotions (e.g., smiling when you are angry, saying it is all right through clenched teeth)?
- Do you get down on your child's level or issue your requests from on high?
- Are most of your conversations happening as you are putting on your coat to go out the door, signaling there is little time to really talk?

- Do people move away or toward you when you are trying to talk with them?
- What are your positive and negative nonverbals?

Now you can expand on your positive or communication-enhancing nonverbals as well as work on eliminating the ones that stop healthy interactions. Changing habits (and ways we protect ourselves) takes time, but the payoff is more ease between you and your loved ones. Now you will go a step further by enlisting their help to learn more about your nonverbals.

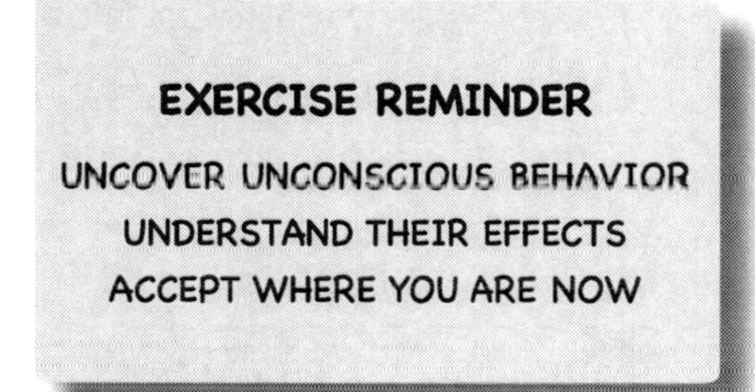

◆ PART 2

Purpose: To learn from your loved ones when and in what way your negative nonverbals appear.

How To: For one day you are going to get some direct feedback from your loved ones. If your children are still very young what will be most helpful is to watch for their reactions. For example, do they seek you out in a relaxed manner or do they cling to you and cry? When you are reunited, do they ask for your reassurance and calm down or do they ignore you? The descriptions about how securely attached children reunite with their parents from Step 3 is also a helpful guide with preverbal children.

With your loved ones you can give some specific instructions to let them know what to do, e.g., "You know how sometimes I have a stern or angry expression on my face or don't look you in the eye when I am talking with you (or another example of what you learned about yourself from Part 1)? I want to change that. Can you help (mommy or daddy) today to know when this is happening? All I ask is that you point it out."

If you have older children, you may want to go through the list above with them and ask for their input – which ones do they see you do and when are they most likely to occur?

Should you be brave enough to do this with older children, you can also practice another important part of communication: simply listening. Take on this job as a reporter or a writer would, getting more background information about an important person. Writing things down can also give you time to process what you hear and to self-soothe if something might trigger you. Don't take what is said too personally, even when there might be some less-than-helpful tones of voice or comments made ("Yeah, you always do that one!" or "I hate it when you raise your voice"). Keep in mind that you are in the process of setting the stage to change the way you communicate with your loved ones. Ask questions for clarification (e.g., "And when am I more likely to roll my eyes?"); this will help you increase your awareness of when negative nonverbals pop out. With your new awareness, practice changing these behaviors on a daily basis, as I'll explain in the next step.

A final caution for this exercise: do not ask your children now how they feel about your nonverbals, as this can be overly challenging. Take it a step at a time. However, at this point you might ask what would work better for them. Also, for your own sake, establish ground rules about appropriate times and how things are said to make it easier to hear what loved ones have to say. Some kids are really going to like this assignment, but telling you in the middle of a store or when you are having a loaded conversation is not the time or place that will make anyone feel better.

Changing Ineffective Nonverbals

Taking one nonverbal at a time, pay attention to what you have learned from your own observation and what others say about how and when it appears. Keeping it in mind, consciously change the behavior. You might give yourself a reward for making this change or you can get loved ones to give you positive feedback for it. I've personally found that my scary 'thoughtful' face occurs less and less as I am paying more attention to my automatic responses and the positive feedback I get from others who no longer look distressed when we talk!

Now you are ready to learn more about effective communication in the next and final step; healthy talking and listening.

CHAPTER 9

Step 9:
The Talk: Healthy Talking and Listening

"The most basic of all human needs is the need to understand and be understood. The best way to understand people is to listen to them." —Ralph G. Nichols

In addition to having a good grasp on nonverbals and techniques that comfortably open conversations, every parent needs effective speaking and listening skills. In this Step you will find many ideas about good communication, most of which are based on Dr. Thomas Gordon's "Parent Effectiveness Training," originally published in 1970. This book is still in print 45 years later because it is so helpful for parents seeking to communicate better and to reach their goal of raising healthy and happy children.

For our work regarding sexuality and relationships, we will start with what Gordon identifies as roadblocks to communication, specifically "put-down messages." I have added a few others that are additional roadblocks.

Conversation-killing Approaches

In the following are thirteen common roadblocks that stall connecting with your kids. Note the examples of how parents deliver these killers and see what, if any, fit you.

1. Judging, Criticizing, Blaming

"If you keep on this way, you'll ruin your life."
"You must have led him on..."
"What's wrong with you?"

2. Name-calling, Ridiculing, Shaming

"You're dressed like a slut!"
"I'm ashamed of you. I can't even look at you right now."
"You're acting gay."

3. Interpreting, Diagnosing, Psychoanalyzing

"I can see what you really wanted to do with that boy."
"You're boy-crazy now, but you'll get over it."
"Your hormones are raging, that's why you feel like this now."
"This is just a phase. You're not really gay/lesbian/trans, etc."

4. Teaching, Instructing

"When I was your age, these were the rules of dating."
"When you're older you'll understand, but you aren't old enough yet."
"Listen to me. I know better than you."

5. Commanding

"I don't ever want to hear you say something like that again!"

"We'll tell you what's good for you."

"Don't you get pregnant!"

6. Prophesying/Doom-saying

"You'll end up just like your no-good (fill in the blank)."

"You're just like your (father/mother). You'll never learn how to really love someone."

7. Disappearing/Passing the buck

"Go ask your (mother, father)."

"You can learn about that at school."

"Just wait until your (father, mother) gets home."

8. Teasing in public/violating privacy

"See how cute your friend, Sara, looks now? You could try harder."

"Show your friends a picture of that girl you are dating. She is hot!"

"I saw your text messages. Do you think he (or she) likes you?"

"I told your father (mother, aunt, my friends) what you told me."

9. Abetting

"Now there are some girls who will put out, but they are not the ones you get in a relationship with."

"Look at a little porn to learn what you should do during sex."

"You can steal any guy you want if you know how."

10. **Averting or Comparing**

"That is not part of this discussion."

"What can't you be a good girl like (your sister, your friend)?"

"Let's talk about that some other time."

11. **Perpetuating Gender Stereotypes**

"Women only care about how much money a man makes."

"Men are biologically programmed to cheat."

"Only sissies cry. Stop that now!"

"Girls don't really mean no when they say it."

12. **Perpetuating Love/Relationship Stereotypes**

"Teens can't really know what love is."

"Love can conquer any problem."

"If you are too successful (or smart), you'll never get a man."

13. **Enforcing heteronormativity**

"You just need to give girls (or boys) a chance."

"You'll grow out of this phase and meet some nice girl (or boy)."

"You're too young to know who you are attracted to."

Keep in mind that you don't have to be perfect or like everything your child does or says. The key here is the approach you take to sharing your thoughts and fears. Some parents believe that to show unconditional love means they should never share anything that might be considered negative, but that is not realistic either. The definition of unconditional love that I favor is this: "The choice we make to feel love for another person even in the face of disappointments or situations." This does not mean acceptance with no boundaries of what others do; rather it means to act consciously and with love in our interpersonal relationships. While you may have strong feelings about how girls or boys should act, you can replace judging, shaming, instructing, or name-calling with a thoughtful consideration about how you want to impart your values to your child in a loving and clear way.

Our first step here is a crucial one: willingness to listen and to do so wholeheartedly. As Gordon puts it, parents need to create a language of acceptance so children will talk with you (and listen). To do that you must be aware of the automatic triggers you have that make communication impossible. By identifying what they are, you can start to change them.

EXERCISE REMINDER

RECOGNIZE YOUR ROADBLOCKS
AFFIRM RESOLVE TO CHANGE
PRACTICE ALTERNATIVES

Exercise: Identifying and Changing Roadblocks

PURPOSE: Identifying communication roadblocks and discovering ways to change them.

HOW TO: Go back to the list of roadblocks above. First, note the categories that describe your current communication behaviors. For each one, mark examples from the list that you are using and add ones that are unique to you.

Next, examine each statement and investigate the sources. Most likely, you learned to make statements like this from your own growing-up years, criticisms you have internalized, abuse you may have endured, and a desire to be the perfect parent to the outside world. They may also come from your desire to protect your child, or to avoid embarrassment, anxiety, anger, or, even more commonly, fear.

Certainly there are other factors to consider. It is possible that making statements like these in fact do come from being judgmental, having poor boundaries or a lack of respect for your children, or, even, due to some problems with mental illness including your own experiences of abuse or neglect. You might talk like this to your kids when you have had too much to drink or the use of some other substance. If any of these are true for you, you may feel some guilt or shame about them; in this case I strongly advise talking to a mental health professional or taking part in a professional treatment group to heal shame and guilt so that they no longer damage your relationships.

If you are able to identify a trigger that lies behind your

roadblock, it is helpful to keep that in mind as you move forward. However it isn't unusual for nothing specific to come to mind. Growing up, all of us learn so many things from many people and events; it isn't necessary to spend much time attempting to find a specific link. It is enough for now for you to make a list of the types of roadblocks you use or fear that you might.

To better understand what to do next, let's look at a specific example. Please note that the gender of any of the people in this scenario could be different and the problems would still be the same.

Getting Called to the Principal's Office

Valerie, age ten, was sent to the principal's office because her teacher intercepted a note she had tried to give in class to one of her friends. The note had some drawings of both male and female genitalia on it and words to describe the drawings like "pussy" and "dick." When Valerie's mother, Shawna, got to school, she was already steamed up about having to leave work and a little scared of what her daughter might have done. Being called into the principal's office brought back memories of the time when her own mother had to come to school because her daughter had been caught taking a girl's notebook.

As Shawna entered the room she sees her daughter looking miserable and refusing to make eye contact. Shawna then assumed her daughter must have done something re-

ally bad to act this way and she finds herself fighting some panic and anger. When the principal explained what Valerie had done, Shawna immediately told him that this behavior was inexcusable and that she would punish Valerie at home.

Valerie attempted to explain what had happened, but her mother said to stop talking and go get in the car. On the way home, Shawna, who had been embarrassed by the look on the principal's face, began the lecture. "What were you thinking? How could you shame our family like that? What's wrong with you? People are going to think you are a slut! No daughter of mine will talk like that! Wait until I tell your father about this!" On and on it went. Once again Valerie tried to explain, but her mother talked over her, yelled at her, and threatened that she would ground her for the next month. When they got home Shawna immediately blurted out what had happened to her husband, James, while Valerie stood there with a miserable look on her face. Making matters worse for them all, James actually started laughing and told Shawna to calm down and get over it; all kids do these things. Valerie ran to her room and slammed the door.

This is obviously a dicey situation for both the parent and the girl. Developmentally, we have a girl who is moving toward puberty and is no doubt curious about body parts. However, we don't know if the drawing was hers or if she was giving it back to her friend. If she did do the drawing, what was the source of her "inspiration?" Shawna was both irritated and a bit fearful going into this situation. She didn't stop to ask her daughter her version of what happened; instead, she immediately says she will take care of the "situation." When Valerie attempts to speak on the way home, her mother doesn't listen, preferring to lecture, shame, gender stereotype, and name-call. Her husband's laughter undermines his wife by not listening. Valerie, now shut out of explaining herself to either parent, flees the scene.

How could using our Steps handle this situation?

Team work

- Parents can confer with each other before one of goes to meet with the principal (mobilize their daughter's support team).
- Rather than relying on one parent to always be responsible for managing problems with the child, choose the best parent for the job. If one parent is more likely to remain calm in these situations, that person should make every attempt to be present.

Your story and self-soothing or grounding

- Identify any personal triggers that being called to the principal's office brings up in you and mindfully calm your fears.
- On the way to the school, don't assume the worst about your child and continue to practice self-soothing while telling yourself you don't know the whole story. Think of one quality about your child you admire. Think of an example of how your child lives that quality and keep a loving image of the

child in mind as you go to the appointment.

- After hearing what the school official has to say, ask for time to speak with your child privately before making any promises or decisions. This allows for your child to be heard and there is more time to calm down.

Focus on nonverbals

- Upon entering the office, concentrate on using positive nonverbal behavior, such as looking your daughter in the eye to make some positive contact with her before greeting the principal.
- Make physical contact with your child to show regard, hold her hand or put your hand on her shoulder.
- Keep your body open to both people in the room, including your child.

Be in a Listening Mode

- Listen fully to the principal before jumping in to defend or apologize.
- Show respect for your child by calmly asking her to explain in her own words what happened.

Use Knowledge to Assess the Issue

- Is what happened developmentally appropriate for your child's age? It is normal to be curious about bodies and there is no reason to feel shamed by what might have happened.

Healthy communication skills of your team

- Make time at home for everyone to be ready to talk together.

- Discuss possible actions to take after listening to your child; meet with child to acknowledge responsibility and discuss any consequences.
- Give a response to the school administrators that is balanced.

Values

- Consider respect for the teacher and class time that was lost from passing notes.
- Consider the family's values about curiosity and sexual topics.
- If appropriate, discuss the limits of friendship with your child.

Your preparation work will make handling these types of happenings in your child's life less about reaction and more about healthy action.

Exercise: Identify Your Triggers and Reactions

PURPOSE: To uncover reactions you may have to routine interactions with your child that result in ineffective nonverbal and verbal communication.

HOW TO: If your children are school age and you had a conflict with one of them recently, go back to the beginning of that day. Identify the factors that might have led to the conflict or its escalation, such as your being tired, hung over, stressed, sick, hungry, or emotionally upset.

Next, consider what your verbal and nonverbal body language was like, such as turning away, making a face, yelling, or showing anger. Did you use any roadblocks such as lecturing, name-calling, avoiding, or criticizing? While the child may indeed have been acting petulant, disrespectful, or talking back, in the end the only one you have control over is you. Consider how your child's behavior might trigger you, and how you can keep your focus on your reactions and actions instead of losing control.

Prepare for the next conflict by planning one thing you can change in your action or reaction. Each time you change even one behavior it puts you on the way to opening the door to better communication. Go back over your example to see if you can pick out any patterns (typical triggers, time of day, etc.) and determine where you could put your parenting tools into play. These might include being aware of any personal issues going on for you, such as stress at work. Then identify ways your co-parent or support system can assist you during your more stressful times. Finally, make a list of what might you have done differently, such as uncrossing your arms, taking a deep breath, having a snack, being mindfully in contact with your child, etc.

Verbal Acceptance

Learning to listen from a position of interested attention is a crucial skill for parents to develop. When people aren't really listening it is usually because they are thinking about what to say in response or they have rushed into responding already. Let's continue with Valerie and her parents to see some of the ways parents respond verbally that are a guaranteed to have a negative impact on their children, leading them to believe their parents don't accept them.

James has gone to Valerie's room and, giving her a little smile, says, "Hey, dinner's ready. What do you want for dessert?" Valerie comes downstairs and sits sullenly at the table. Shawna and James are mostly talking with each other, catching up on their respective days, but neither one of them is looking at Valerie. This goes on for about fifteen minutes while Valerie pushes her food around her plate. Suddenly her mother tells her to stop sulking and eat. Valerie blurts out, "You can't make me eat if I'm not hungry!" James replies, "If you keep talking to your mother like that, I'll send you to your room with no dinner." Valerie rolls her eyes and her mother tells her to stop acting like a brat.

After another five minutes of eating in silence, Shawna and James begin to clear the table and tell Valerie they are ready to talk to her about what happened at school. Valerie stares at her hands and Shawna asks, Did you make that drawing?" Valerie silently nods her head. Her mother then says, "Where did you even get the idea to do such a thing? Where did you learn language like that?" Before Valerie can even answer, James jumps in and asks, "Did you do it so the other kids would like you? I bet that's it." Shawna shoots a look at her husband and says, "I don't care why she did it. She isn't showing respect for us or her teacher with this kind of behavior." The parents start to bicker between themselves about who is right and meanwhile, Valerie hasn't said anything. As she watches them argue she gets more and more agitated; finally she jumps up and shouts, "I hate you two. You never listen to me." and she storms off again to her room.

In reviewing this scenario, it is obvious what the parents are doing is not effective. In P.E.T., Gordon describes what he calls the "typical twelve." These are twelve common ways parents respond to their child's communication.

1. **Ordering, Directing, Commanding** – telling the child to do something, giving him an order or command.
2. **Warning, Admonishing, Threatening** – telling the child what consequences will occur if she does something.
3. **Exhorting, Moralizing, Preaching** – telling the child what he should or ought to do.
4. **Advising, Giving Solutions or Suggestions** – telling the child how to solve a problem, giving her advice or suggestions; providing answers or solutions for her.
5. **Lecturing, Teaching, Giving Logical Arguments** – trying to influence the child with facts, counter-arguments, logic, information, or your own opinions.
6. **Judging, Criticizing, Disagreeing, Blaming** – making a negative judgment or evaluation of the child.
7. **Praising, agreeing** – offering a positive evaluation or judgment; agreeing.
8. **Name-calling, Ridiculing, Shaming** – making the child feel foolish, putting the child into a category; shaming her.

9. **Interpreting, Analyzing, Diagnosing** - telling the child what his motives are or analyzing why he is doing or saying something; communicating that you have figured out or have him diagnosed.
10. **Reassuring, Sympathizing, Consoling, Supporting** - trying to make the child feel better, talking her out of her feelings, trying to make her feelings go away, denying the strength of her feelings.
11. **Probing, Questioning, Interrogating** - trying to find the reasons, motive, causes; searching for more information to help you solve the problem.
12. **Withdrawing, Distracting, Humoring, Diverting** - trying to get the child away from the problem; withdrawing from the problem yourself; distracting the child, kidding him out of it, pushing the problem aside.

Let's see which of these typical twelve are going on in the second scenario with Valerie and her parents. James opens up the scenario with #12 - *Withdrawing, Distracting, Humoring, Diverting*. He isn't acknowledging Valerie's nonverbal behavior and he tries to distract her with what she wants for dessert. Both parents also withdraw from the problem by focusing on themselves and ignoring the elephant in the room. Valerie's non-verbal eating behavior elicits #1 from her mother, *Ordering, Directing, Commanding*. When Valerie fights back with a rebellious comment, her father issues a #2, *Warning, Admonishing, Threatening*. In response to Valerie's eye-rolling (a sign of contempt), her mother resorts to #3, *Exhorting, Moralizing, Preaching*. When the discussion about the school incident actually starts, Shawna begins with #11, *Probing, Questioning, Interrogating*. Before Valerie can even answer her mother's interrogation, her father pulls out # 9, *Interpreting, Analyzing, Diagnosing*. Then the parents start bickering between themselves and ignore their daughter (an issue of their communication with each other). With her daughter forced to listen, Shawna uses Exhorting, Moralizing, Preaching in her argument with her husband.

It's exhausting for everyone in this scenario and they accomplish nothing. Neither parent was actually listening and both ignored Valerie's verbal and nonverbal signals of her distress. In this kind of situation it is important to create what Gordon calls "door-openers." Basically, these are actions or phrases designed to invite your child to talk with you. They convey respect for your child's thoughts, feelings, and opin ions as well as your interest in them.

Door openers include remaining silent so that others have room to speak, encouraging nonverbals such as nodding your head or a thoughtful expression, and noncommittal responses such as "hmmm" and "okay," and "I see." Some phrases are extremely useful in this: "Tell me more about that," "Would you like to talk about it," and "This sounds like something important to you." You may well know all of these, but people tend to forget them when anxious, fearful, or put on the spot.

The Role of Listening

Active listening is another tool to encourage children to talk. Even though it is an old technique and may feel somewhat artificial at first, it is remarkably effective. Active listening means hearing what the other person says, thinking about what the other person may be feeling or the message he or she wants to convey, and feeding back that decoded message to check for accuracy.

For example, your child says, "I hate my teacher! He is always harder on me and he doesn't like me, I just know it! I'm not going back to school ever again and you can't make me!" The parent, not trying to correct the child or talk them out of what they are saying, says something like this, "You are very upset about your teacher and you feel like you feel so strongly about it you don't ever want to return. Did I get that right?" Should the child say that the parent didn't get it., he or she can ask more questions ("Can you tell me more so I can understand what you are saying") and attempt another decoding. By doing this, the parent is not agreeing or disagreeing with the child's perceptions and feelings, he or she is showing that they heard what was being shared.

Another beauty of active listening is that you can use it as a way to self-soothe. Instead of blurting out a roadblock, parents can use the formula to provide themselves time to think and to listen. To build more trust in your child's decision-making skills, practice actually wanting to hear what your child has to say. **Bonus:** your children learn to express positive and negative emotions and to develop a more secure attachment as they experience greater acceptance of their feeling and thoughts.

Managing Failures to Communicate With Your Child

You will get much more respect and support for what you are trying to change when your partner and children see you are actively trying. For example, I often catch myself in the middle of doing something my family members don't like, which I can tell by their expression or the direction the conversation is going. I stop myself and say something like, "Can we start over?" or "Let me try that again a different way." If things fall apart or end badly, I go off and self-soothe to keep from defending myself or from picking apart what the other person said or did. I also review my list of conversation killers and roadblocks. Once I am clear about what I did and what I need to change, I go back to my partner or child to see if we can try again. This time I remind myself to slow things down, and to listen more than talk.

This way of handling communication glitches also models for children how to be authentic and aware when difficult conversations erupt or go awry. When you need to talk with them about tricky topics, your previous behavior will have shown them how to listen more effectively themselves.

Of course, as with any relationship, you may not get the response or the behavior you would like. This can be challenging, but consistently using door-openers and actively listening will help your loved ones better communicate with you and others. If you help them feel safe about expressing their emotions and thoughts, it will be much less likely that they will resort to defensiveness, blame, or petulance. Your relationships will deepen and you will feel more peaceful and resilient as a parent and a partner.

Conclusions

None of us come to parenting completely equipped to handle some of the more vexing issues in raising children. Using these steps, parents can feel empowered to talk with their children about difficult topics like sexuality and relationships. My hope is that you now feel empowered and prepared to continue your own education about sexuality and relationships so you can use the skills presented in this book.

CHAPTER 10

Creating Healthy Family and Community Interactions

"When you invite people to share in your miracle, you create future allies during rough weather."
—Shannon L. Alder

As the above quote says so well, having a team to support you in parenting is key to easing the bumps and demands that all parents face. In this chapter you will find information and tips about how to put your own team together with the other important people in your child's life. These might include new partners or spouses, extended family and friends, foster parents and group-home staff, child-care workers, school personnel, medical/mental health staff, and religious groups.

New Partners/Spouses

At least 33% of children will live in a blended family at some point in their life, from birth to age 18. Couples face many challenges in this situation. These include one partner not having children; the age of the children involved; the other parent in the child's life; how long the parents have been divorced; if there was a death of a parent and how long ago it occurred; extended family, and different parenting styles.

The first task I recommend for parents with a blended family is that both partner/spouses read and follow the Steps in this book. Doing so will allow you to acknowledge any differences in parenting styles and work together to establish your new team. The Steps also involve such important factors as being curious about your partner's world, listening deeply and asking questions, and sharing your hopes and dreams. They will help you clearly understand the boundaries in your joint parenting and prevent children from playing one parent off the other.

When it comes to discipline and setting rules, the biological or adoptive parent should take the lead at first. As time goes on, the new partner can begin to share aspects of the parental role as well. Pacing it in this manner will produce better outcomes for children and the couple. Children need time to grieve the loss of their first family or the way in which they were first raised, as well as time to form a bond with the parent's new partner or spouse.

Of course that is just one of the complications that arise in blended families. The other parent of the child might have different ideas about handling sex and relationship education, plus there may well be unresolved ill will, anger, and resentment about the breakup or divorce. It is important that all the adults involved talk with one another in order to create the most caring environment for the children and strive to be civil and even supportive of the new blended group. Obviously, if major tensions remain between former partners it puts the stepparent at more of a disadvantage and creates strife that can undermine and even breakup the new relationship.

As tough as it may be, unless they get their act together, adults in this situation can't do what is in the best interests of the children. This means letting go of anger and resentment, not putting others down, and working to allow the children to grow up with low stress around the adults in their lives. A good deal of research backs up how crucial this is; it points to a long list of negative outcomes for children when the adults around them are fighting, actively nasty about and to one another, or doing whatever they can to make the former partner's life miserable. If you are still angry and resentful, please get professional help. Resentments mainly hurt the person who has them, but in this case, the children and your new relationship will also suffer.

Family Rules in Blended Families

Developing family rules is crucial to creating more trust and harmony. If both partners in the new couple are bringing children into the blended family, you can see the conflicts that can arise from different parenting styles including about sex and relationships. For example, one parent might stress providing children with resources and education, while the other parents involved don't want their children to have them. Children are going to talk among themselves, which makes it impossible to give information to one child and keep it from the other(s). If children move between two houses, it may be the stepparent who is present and may feel stuck in what to say or do when a life event happens that the child needs information about.

In the following are a few examples of situations related to sexuality and relationships that require all adults involved to develop family rules. Add more to the list that fit for your particular family.

- Privacy rules
- Accessibility of books and resources about sexuality
- Internet rules
- Media consumption
- Who and how will pubertal milestones like starting menstruation or having a wet dream be handled
- Sharing bedrooms with step-siblings
- Dating

Children can handle some difference in the rules between houses, but having a lot of divergence combined with conflict will cause greater struggles for them concerning loyalty and negative emotions.

I can't stress enough how important it is for you and your partner to have clear communication and to extend it to the other parent as well. Stepparents can be put in risky situations when, for instance, their stepchildren or their partner's children ask them about sexuality or intimate relationships. Children are likely to repeat what they hear at one home to the other parent involved and it can carry risk for stepparents. The possibility exists that they could be accused of improper contact with the child or teen with the result that the other parent limits visitation based on a stepparent's actions. An innocent but misconstrued conversation could even alienate their own partner who feels they've overstepped their bounds.

The advice I have here applies to most blended family situations in which the adults involved are mentally healthy and treat one another with respect.

1. The partner and stepparent must discuss together what is expected of the stepparent concerning questions about sexuality and intimate relationships. Make a plan for how best to handle most situations. The parent of the children must consider deeply how to include the new partner in a healthy way, and abide by a rule never to criticize him or her in front of the children.
2. Stepparents must always let the parent know when the child has asked a question of them and understand that the partner will need to let the other parent know about it as well. Children

must also know that the stepparent will talk with the parent about the conversation. Never have secrets. (Again, I stress this unless there is a parent who is mentally ill or where some kind of domestic violence or abuse is occurring – get professional help!)

3. As a stepparent, don't expect too much too soon from the children newly in your life; keep your partner informed as your relationships change.
4. If both partners are bringing children into the relationship and there are different rules, adults will need to be clear to the children concerning that. The rules could be about dating, driving, Internet use, access to birth control, etc. In this case, you can't expect the children to like that there are different rules or think it is fair. However, by explaining to them that the two of you might have different opinions and being clear about the wishes of the other parents involved, you are modeling behaviors for the children. They can see that adults don't always agree but that they can continue to talk with one another openly.

In researching the literature and the internet for what blended families might do around the area of sex and relationships education, I was a bit shocked to find virtually nothing. Consequently, I have based my recommendations on what research literature findings show result in the best general outcomes for blended families. The most important factor for all the adults in your child's life, regardless of varied decisions, is to maintain clear communication at all times.

Extended Family and Friends

Having an extended family brings with it many benefits such as the wisdom and the knowledge others can bring, getting a break from childcare, or having time together as a couple when grandparents or other relatives step in to babysit. The connection of extended families can offer an invaluable sense of belonging and security.

On the downside, when it comes to sexuality and relationships, extended families often have different attitudes, beliefs, and behaviors. Grandparents or older members in the family may feel it is their role to ensure that the children learn religious and cultural norms and, in some cases, they become the enforcers of them. When extended family members take on childcare, it may result in blurring of parental rules that create conflict and confusion. As the parent of the children you may fear what the parents/grandparents or other relatives might think about how you teach your children regarding sex and relationships. In a blended family, the new partner or spouse will bring his or her extended family into the mix as well.

In the case of relatives living with your family, you will need to use the communication skills you have learned in this book to talk about your expectations and values. Ask your relatives about their education, experiences, fears, and expectations as well. Be clear with them about what sources of information you prefer for your children and how family members can help in what you want discussed with your child. Don't shy away from letting them know how you want to handle differences of values and how important their respect and support is to you as you parent your children.

Don't be surprised if your parents are more with it about sexuality and relationships than they were when they were raising you. Even though my mother didn't offer me much in the way of healthy sex education when I was growing up, I loved watching her sit with my daughter and giggle through some of the sex education books I had in the house. Give your family the opportunity to be there for you.

Foster Parents/Group Home Staff

About 400,000 children are in an out-of-home placement on any given day in the United States, which includes family settings and settings like group homes. Typically, children are in foster care because of child abuse and/or neglect, or because there are some kinds of special family circumstances. Safety is paramount for those caring for the children of others. Those who open their homes to children as foster parents, as well as group-home organizations, must follow a long list of regulations, rules, and laws while caring for children. While these vary from state to state, many of the rules are designed to maintain clear boundaries and include behavioral approaches that alter normal parenting behaviors. Some of these rules are about touching, what kinds of clothing must be worn outside of the bedroom, who can share bedrooms, what to do about wrestling, tickling, playing doctor, etc. If a child is known to have been sexually abused, rules may be specific regarding how foster parents can comfort the child.

Other guidelines for foster homes and group homes might cover having the child understand that there can be no sexual play or sexual touching, no masturbation around others, no sexualized language or behaviors, and no bringing inappropriate sexually related materials into the home. In the case of someone making inappropriate sexual touching, the children need to know they must report it to the foster parent and other appropriate adults. This supposes that the child is clear about what all these things mean and feels safe to talk about them.

Foster parents do get considerable training about how to handle the rules, regulations, and emotional needs of their foster children, but rarely do foster-care or group-home agencies provide these important adults sex education. In most states, foster parents and staff in group homes are mandated to report any suspected child abuse or neglect. Understandably adults in charge may be reluctant to talk about any matters related to sexuality with a child, in some cases to avoid re-traumatizing the child, but also to avoid having to do a mandated report. It is beyond the scope of this book to get into this kind of training, but I encourage people who work in social service and mental health not to avoid the topic of sex. You may be the only person a child will start to trust. I believe all of us in these fields have an opportunity to make a big difference here.

Foster parents will find that when giving information to a child, much depends on his or her cognitive capacity and placement circumstances. For example, in voluntary placements, you are allowed to consult with biological parents and family members. To find out what information pertains in your situation, start by checking with your social worker. When I do trainings with foster parents, I counsel them to document all conversations about sexuality and the times that they, as the foster parents, deliver sex education. This is for your protection as well as the child in your care.

You will find resources in Chapter 11 regarding sex education for children who have been traumatized in some way, including physical and sexual abuse or assault, as well as neglect. All children have the right to learn about healthy, positive sexuality and intimate relationships. This is a big part of the hard work of being a parent or foster parent.

One problem in the system is that not all professionals in it are educated equally. While social workers are expected to understand child and adolescent development in general terms, this does not mean they have had extensive sex education themselves. Unfortunately, this is also true for therapists. My work with children and teens in group-home settings showed me that staff members do understand their legal job requirements. However, with respect to the trauma the children with whom they work may have experienced, staff members are often ill trained to understand their needs, much less the sex and relationship education that would be appropriate for them. My hope is that the steps and resources in this book will help guide foster parents and others who work with these children and prompt requests for more training.

Child Care and School Settings

Childcare workers are also mandated reporters of child abuse and neglect. They must have some kind of formal training in understanding types of child abuse and neglect, recognizing the usual signs, and how to go about making a report. Additional training includes how to minimize risk, what to do if another childcare worker or teacher is alleged to have abused a child or teen, and how to assist the family, perhaps through helping them find resources in the community. However, as with most adults, few childcare workers have formal training in sex education and all of them have their own experiences, attitudes, and values. There are divergent ideas about what is appropriate sexual behavior, especially for children, and adults often send them mixed messages. When a child is in childcare a preschool daycare, he or she will also be introduced to children with different norms of behavior or different experiences. So, what can parents do?

For information on this, I consulted a professional who has been in the business for over 10 years. Here are her suggestions.

- Learn about normal sexual development; this way you will have fewer surprises and assumptions about the behavior of your children and the children of others.
- Interview the staff members in the daycare center you have chosen for your child. What training do they have? How are they instructed to respond when children are sexually curious?
- Ask questions about the broader daycare community; for example, do parents interact with one another outside the center? This can be important if another parent observes your child exhibiting normal curiosity or perhaps fondling his or her crotch during nap or movie time, and chats about it to other parents.
- If you are a GBLT parent, how will the daycare staff respect you and how will the daycare community respond? Will the daycare staff be supportive and inclusive?

Here are what she would like parents to know and do when possible.

- Let staff members know if you have specific requests about your child's sex education. Children ask questions of the staff throughout the day. Given that there is limited privacy, they see other children being changed or using the bathroom, and they will be naturally curious.

- When your child asks something about sexuality, tell the staff how you want them to handle it. Do you want them to text or otherwise consult you?
- When your child asks a question about sex, or other children report some sexual behavior, stay calm. Do not freak out with the staff, your children, or the children of others.
- Above all, don't shame other children and don't ask the staff to do so about behaviors you might not find acceptable in your own child.
- Since people will have different values and expectations of their child; don't judge or make assumptions that a child's curiosity about sex means something like sexual abuse must have happened.
- Avoid talking about other children and his or her parents except to the staff. Discuss with them first if you have concerns.
- Finally, if your child has an abuse or trauma history, it can be helpful for the owner or head staff person to know about it. Admittedly, doing so can feel tricky for parents for several reasons. They may not want to be judged and they likely would not want their child's overall behavior to be viewed through a particular lens. They might also be concerned that the information would not stay confidential.

Safety is the primary focus of childcare workers; having some knowledge of the special experience or needs of your child will add them to the team to ensure his or her safety. While confidentiality should be a given, be clear when asking how the owner will keep your confidence and use the information in your child's care.

School Personnel

As is true with all professional groups I have discussed thus far, school personnel receive basic education in child development as well as the ethical and legal aspects of their jobs as mandated reporters. Once again, most school personnel will not have had formal sex education and may not have adequate knowledge to do what is best for your child. Their attitudes and beliefs will also affect how they interact with your child. Even so, teachers and other school personnel may be wary about what they say to students regarding questions about sexuality or gender because of the potential reactions of colleagues or parents. The age of the children may also play a role with more acceptance and support for younger children's curiosity and behavior than for that of tweens and older children.

For parents of a child who falls outside what society deems as typical gender-specific behavior, it is wise to meet with school officials. Public school systems are supposed to create a place of safety for all children, but with respect to gender variance, school districts' rules and attitudes vary widely across the country.

Meeting with your child's principal and teacher is a first

step, but you will need to be aware of other staff members such as nurses or paraprofessionals, as well as parent volunteers in the classroom. Bathroom use has become an issue in some places; again, working out alternatives with the staff that will minimize confusion and teasing for your child is critical for mental and physical health of him or her. The NEA (National Education Association) suggests that teachers be allowed to include lessons plans that underscore human diversity and teach tolerance. However, not all schools or school personnel will be supportive or helpful; make yourself aware of your state's laws and check out the resources in the next chapter for support and help.

As children move toward tween years and puberty, their sexual orientation may become more apparent to them, even if it goes without comment. Because our society typically assumes heterosexuality, other students may marginalize, harass or bully a child who is not seen to have heteronormative interests. Giving children thorough and positive sex education, including respecting themselves and others, will be important to help them protect their sense of self in hostile situations. For parents, taking an active role in school activities or parent-school organizations is a good way to have an influence on the school environment for your child.

By reading the student handbook for your child's school you can find what areas to focus on to provide the healthiest atmosphere for your child. Schools sometimes have dress codes and even rules about whom students can ask to a school dance or prom. Some schools now have clubs, such as a gay-straight alliance, to provide places for all students to feel safe expressing who they are in terms of sexual orientation, gender identity, or being in a questioning place. Such clubs may sponsor school activities to educate teachers and staff as well as other students about what it means to be LGBTQ. As with gender diversity, attitudes and laws are changing across the U.S., but that may not yet be true in your area.

Medical Personnel

Sadly, medical personnel receive little training in human sexuality. They may not know how to ask about a patient's sex life or how treatments and medications might affect sexual functioning or desire. For the most part doctors consider these issues low priority or simply ignore them altogether. Adding to the problem, medical personnel have little input about considering their own attitudes and beliefs, or how to be respectful of differences with their patients, for example, a child's sexual orientation or gender identity. Religious organizations that provide medical care may preclude discussion of certain treatments and make it difficult or impossible for a child to ask medically necessary questions.

Don't hesitate to ask your child's healthcare provider about training received concerning sexual health, also called sexual medicine in some locales. As your child gets older, discuss his or her expectations of privacy when it comes to their discussions with healthcare professionals. Children need to learn how to talk with healthcare providers about all parts of their body and life including asking questions and providing accurate answers about, say, the number of sexual partners, whom they are sexually active with, what types of sexual behaviors they engage in, and even what to do if they have sexual difficulties (pain, erectile or premature ejaculation problems, vaginal dryness, etc.). In terms of their healthcare rights, prepare your children for the reality that some healthcare providers will have different values and attitudes and may not treat them with respect. To find out more, ask your children straight out if they are happy with the medical care they are currently receiving.

Religious Organizations

It's not unusual for adults to have a limited understanding about their particular religion's teaching concerning sexuality, but as a parent, it is important. Religious leaders and members of your religious community might be telling your child things you do not believe or accept. Their interpretations of the same sacred text might be widely divergent even from one religious leader to the next.

Should your child be gender diverse, gay, lesbian, or bisexual, you will need to examine how it will affect your faith and your participation in your faith organization. For example, by investigating the religious leaders' position about homosexuality before you reveal your own family's experience, it will put you in a better place to avoid hurtful and harmful situations for your family. The path to considering whether you stay the course with your current religion or to make a change in your life is not easy. I encourage you to seek support and information from other parents who have made this journey. PFLAG is one of the resources that may be helpful to you.

Conclusions

In these pages it was possible for me to only scratch the surface concerning the different people and organizations in your and your child's life. Unfortunately, it is common for everyone to go through times when the greater community is not supportive about parental choices. This is where you can apply what you have learned about talking effectively with your children to the other important people in your child's world. Take proactive steps to educate others and provide safe and healthy places for your children to grow up in!

Resources for Blended Families

National Stepfamily Resource Center

http://www.stepfamilies.info

A division of Auburn University with a council of stepfamily experts, this website offers connection to experts, educational resources, law and policy and much more for stepfamilies.

Parents.com

http://www.parents.com/parenting/divorce/blended-families/challenges-of-blended-families/

This national magazine has its own website and a page specifically for stepfamilies.

CHAPTER 11

Nurturing Children Who Don't Fit the "Norm"

"When we least expect it, life sets us a challenge to test our courage and willingness to change; at such a moment, there is no point in pretending that nothing has happened or in saying we are not yet ready. The challenge will not wait. Life does not look back." —Paul Coelho

For parents faced with the challenge of raising children who do not fit what society considers the norm, sex education is likely to be a distant priority. It's understandable, but for these children, it is critical that parents teach them about this important aspect of life, as I will explain shortly. In this chapter the focus is on children who are gender variant, those with congenital or acquired disabilities and medical conditions, and children who have been sexually, physically, or emotionally abused or assaulted.

Sadly, support for parents is often lacking concerning sex and relationship education for children that fit these descriptions. Sometimes parents are exhausted or simply lack the awareness and knowledge they need to provide appropriate and accessible education. In the case of trauma and abuse, parents are often concerned that teaching about sex and relationships could cause further damage. Those whose children are gender variant may struggle with religious and cultural beliefs that do not accept it. This chapter provides support and resources having to do with giving all of these children the education they desperately need.

Getting Started

The first step for parents is to acknowledge that regardless of the particular medical or psychological/developmental/societal challenge, most of these children want to have emotional and physical relationships. These are part of a "normal" life, and that is what they seek – having social interactions, friends, and yes, eventually, lovers. Just like any child, they want to have as much control over their body and life as possible. They want to be able to interact socially with other children their age (and sometimes disability) and to have access to information about sex and intimate relationships. They also want to choose whom they love, regardless of gender. Teens and adult children seek to have their parents see them as sexual beings and to help them build a healthy sense of self by sharing their knowledge and values.

Parents sometimes assume that the nature of physical disability a child might have makes having sex impossible. For example, cerebral palsy might make it appear that the child lacks the mobility or coordination required for physical intimacy. But the point to remember is that by no means does this preclude the child's having interest or desire. In some instances, parents may not realize this; having done so much caretaking they may have unknowingly infantilized their child. Additionally, they may truly wonder if anyone would find their child attractive, given such noticeable physical differences.

Even for children without visible disabilities or chronic illness, parents may be so focused on illness management that they never consider how the physical condition affects their child's body image, sense of self as a sexual being, or actual sexual activity. Adding to the problem, parents may have become so protective that they don't allow their children to date, including when they become adults. What it all comes down to is that providing education and information to these children slips to the bottom of a very long list of concerns.

If you are a parent who has this challenge, please understand that ignoring this area hasn't made you a bad parent and that it's not too late to start. Resources are still limited, but you are already an advocate for your child in many other areas and you can take this one on as well. Our work together here will help you broaden your perspective of your child to include that he or she sees him or herself now – or eventually will -- as an emotional and sexual human being.

In my work in this area, I find that parents feel stymied

about how to provide this education and that they are unsure what material is developmentally appropriate or available. In addition, parents are concerned about how vulnerable their child is or may be. For example, they worry that their child may not remember the guidelines about public vs. private sexual behavior, or they fear that the child (or young adult) will not have appropriate control over emotional and sexual desires. Parents are frequently anxious that their children will be further marginalized if they are considered to be acting in a socially inappropriate way or if they go against norms of gendered behavior and dress. A great fear that parents have is that others will take advantage of their child or harm the child with emotional, physical or sexual abuse or assault.

The Facts

Unfortunately, the sad truth is that people who have a disability or are looked at as different are statistically much more likely to experience some kind of violence, whether domestic violence or sexual abuse and assault. Those with developmental disabilities have some of the higher rates of sexual abuse and assault. On the flip side, people with intellectual disabilities who do not fully understand the concept of consent may commit sexual offenses against others that put them in the criminal justice system or they get in trouble at school or work for sexual harassment.

For women with disabilities sexual and interpersonal

violence is common, with the vast majority of the perpetrators known to the victimized person. The list of perpetrators includes family members, medical staff, residential care staff, personal care attendants, acquaintances, and even those who transport children and adults. In some cases, the victim may not understand what is happening. Other issues include threats to the child or adult if they tell anyone; not having the strength or ability to protect themselves physically; feeling shame (as do many victims), or fearing that they will lose a relationship with that person.

Contributing Factors

A variety of factors play a role when people with disabilities are victimized or have offended others. Chief among them is the lack of access to proper sex education. Others include poor social skills or assertiveness training (leading to powerlessness); truncated social lives, and, for older people, having little or no access to dating or sexual partners. Research shows that children with disabilities consistently have far less knowledge about sexuality than their peers without disabilities. When some sex education has taken place, the focus is generally on what not to do or on protection. As a rule it is also written to portray the norm for heterosexual individuals only (that is, heteronormative).

In some children gender nonconformity appears early in life, setting them up as more likely to face bullying and harassment in the larger world. Abuse of this nature is not just from other children; it can come from teachers, doctors, childcare workers, nursery staff, and other adults with whom the child interacts. LGBT youth suffer from much higher violence and abuse rates than their heterosexually identified or cis-gendered (gender identity corresponds to their biological sex) peers. In 2011, the FBI reported that of all hate crimes reported that year, about 20% were against LGBT people.

Children who have been bullied or abused, sexually or physically, often have great psychological suffering, which may lead to greater use of mind-altering substances and suicidal behavior. Parents must be aware that, with or without a history of trauma, their teens may use alcohol and recreational drugs, just like any other teen or young adult. It is important to educate them about how use of these substances might affect giving or understanding consent and also make them more vulnerable to physical and sexual abuse and assault.

What to Do

Without question, this is all deeply troubling and certainly strengthens the call for action to protect these children. Some victimization occurs because children are not prepared, which parents can do much to change. As discussed in Step 1 [see Chapter1], sexuality and emotional development unfold from birth in children with and without disabilities or gender variance. This makes it ideal for parents to prepare themselves as soon as possible to offer their children accurate and ongoing sex and relationship education. Doing so will both protect and prepare children with disabilities or gender variance to live their lives as fully and as safely as possible.

Next Steps in Sex and Relationship Education

All of the steps in this book will help you prepare yourself to educate and talk with children who are out of the norm. I discuss additional modifications you may need to make for these children later in the chapter; feel free to add others as necessary if they better fit the individual nature of your child.

With respect to sexual and emotional development, most children with medical and mental challenges, as well those who are gender diverse will go through the sequences explained in Step 1. For some, though, these developmental stages may unfold more slowly and emerge at an older age than in children without such issues.

In the following I provide advice about education with respect to specific categories of physical, intellectual, and psychological problems. After that you will find online resources listed by categories of disability or difference.

Developmental/Intellectual Disabilities

Children with developmental or intellectual differences will focus, learn, and remember in ways unique to themselves. What works best is for parents and other educators to present information in concrete fashion, repeat it often and move ahead slowly for maximum effect. Depending on the ability to read, some children may need you to read sex education materials to them and/or use books with illustrations that have simplified explanations.

The following tips and suggestions will help make this process more comfortable. I gathered these from research done with children or teens in this category.

- Be careful about who is giving the children information, when not the parents. Some kids feel more comfortable if they know the person providing information about sex; some may prefer the person to be the same gender as them.
- Don't assume that these children want in-depth sex education at a given age. You will likely find that younger children want to learn certain aspects of it then but have no interest in other areas until later in their life. Stay sensitive to how your child responds to information.
- Be aware that for education in group settings, younger children may prefer same-sex ones, while later in life prefer being in a mixed-gender group.
- Having peers to talk with about things like dating and sexual functioning is something teens really wanted.

Start early and let your child's ability to understand and

react to the information serve as your guide, presenting sex education in stages as appropriate. Children need accurate information as well as your values and an understanding of societally competent behaviors. Your child's non-sexual behaviors may be misconstrued (e.g., prolonged hugging seen as sexual), making it especially important to teach about consent. Be clear in your teachings about masturbation including appropriate places to do this sex-positive behavior – it is imperative to avert legal problems. Because many children on the autism spectrum have sensory sensitivities, parents and educators must pay close attention to the individual child's sensitivities and plan education accordingly.

It may come as a surprise for parents of children on the autism spectrum or with intellectual disabilities to learn that they have a higher rate of gender nonconforming or transgender identity than the general population. (More information on gender nonconforming in a subsequent section.)

Visual Impairment or Blindness

Children who are blind obviously do not have visual experiences that in sighted children can spur conversations, such as seeing a pregnant woman. Using an anatomically correct doll makes it possible to teach about body parts by having your child touch and discuss. For teaching hygiene parents have to be more experiential, providing information through touch and smell, for example.

Given that touch is so important to the visually impaired

or blind, they need clear rules about touching, both in terms of whom and how they touch and who may touch them. Parents must also teach children to close the blinds or shut a door to create privacy, given that they experience this naturally. Being allowed to explore and navigate the world on their own, as appropriate, gives children greater self-confidence and self-sufficiency, which might also lessen some of your worries about a child's vulnerability. Remember, too, as part of this that learning how to put on a condom is as important as how to navigate consent.

Deaf and Hard of Hearing

Children who are deaf or hard of hearing may get no sex education at all or what information is available to them is not in a form they understand. Signing a word for example, vagina -- isn't enough for deaf children; for full understanding they also need to see a graphic or picture. To be useful, videos need to have subtitles. Staff at school for the deaf may not have adequate education themselves, which may be complicated by their embarrassment about using sign language for certain aspects of sexuality.

Again, though, in spite of the hindrances, adequate sex education is crucial for deaf children. Without it they might not fully understand a sexual advance or misconstrue it as something else. This puts children at greater risk for abuse and assault. Making the problem more difficult, children and teens may not have adequate vocabulary to describe what happened and finding therapists who are trained to work with the deaf population is very difficult.

Physical Disabilities

Many different types of conditions can be included in this category. Some conditions may be present from birth such as spina bifida, muscular dystrophy, or cerebral palsy. These can affect neurological functioning resulting in problems with mobility, muscle weakness, and spastic muscle movement. Developmental delays, seizures, and problems with vision, hearing, and speech may occur. Children born with dwarfism or of short stature can have problems with joint flexibility and degeneration, as well as chronic pain. These conditions can interfere with normal sexual functioning making an increased need for more information about alternatives than what is in the average sex education book.

Other physical disabilities, such as spinal cord injuries that affect movement and sensation, may be acquired later in life. Adults can find guidelines that discuss sexual functioning after spinal cord injury, but there is little basic sex education to help children and teens with spinal cord inury to navigate normal sexual development. How the injury or congenital conditions might affect sexual functioning is dependent on the location and degree of it. For example, while feeling may be limited or absent with spinal cord injures, boys will still be able to get an erection and even ejaculate. Both males and females may be able to orgasm, although the specific feeling may be altered or absent. This can be vital information in their interpersonal relationships as they grow up.

Experiencing incontinence or needing caretakers can affect many aspects of a child's life and make the transition to having more intimate social and sexual experiences difficult. This means parents and educators have to be inventive when discussing possibilities for sexual pleasure and varieties of ways of achieving it.

Keep in mind always that children with physical disabilities will want answers as to how their physical condition might affect their sexuality and reproductive lives. Some conditions will eventually call for genetic counseling to determine if this is something they could pass on to their offspring.

Chronic illness/physical health

Some chronic illness may be the result of a genetic abnormality (e.g., sickle cell anemia or cystic fibrosis). Others (juvenile diabetes, asthma) may develop in childhood or in adolescence/young adulthood (Type 1 or 2 diabetes, lupus, epilepsy, multiple sclerosis). Of course, some illnesses such as cancer can develop at any age.

Depending on the type and course of the illness and as well as the treatment necessary to manage it, a child might be at risk for a number of issues. These include: delayed growth and puberty, altered body image, lack of self-efficacy, mobility challenges, medication side effects, depression and loneliness leading to use of drugs and alcohol. Medical crises may result in missing school or needing to be home-schooled, thereby limiting social development. At school, children may face ignorance and bullying with even teachers or staff responding inappropriately to them.

A desire to have control of their life, to fit in, and to be seen as "normal" may lead children to taking greater risks than peers without chronic illnesses. These risks include using drugs and alcohol, which can put people at more risk for unwanted or unprotected sex, as well as engaging in sexual behaviors to please or keep a partner. Thus, parents need to provide education and support for them to develop a strong knowledge base, a sense of self efficacy, good decision-making skills and opportunities to engage in social interactions with their peers. As difficult as it may be for some parents to think about, adolescents will need access to birth control. Hopefully you have developed your team with family, friends, and health professionals you can recruit as resources to help you in strengthening your child's emotional and sexual education.

Mental Illness

The category of mental illnesses encompasses a fairly large number of possibilities. I am focusing on specific mental illnesses such as mood (depression, bipolar disorder) or anxiety disorders (generalized anxiety disorder, specific phobias), attention deficit-hyperactivity disorders and psychotic illnesses such as schizophrenia. Parents may face other types of mental illnesses, but my intent here is to provide just a brief overview of considerations concerning the sex and relationship education of your children.

Of course, children or teens who exhibit significant symptoms of any of these mental illnesses need professional help. If a child or teen is actively psychotic, their safety and that of others is paramount. The education of children with mental illnesses about normal sex and relationships takes place in times of remission and is done as with any child. An important difference is that many psychotropic medications have sexual side effects, which include loss of desire, interference with erection and delays in orgasm/ejaculation. Indeed, people in their late teens and into adult years frequently stop taking their medications because of sexual side effects and weight gain associated with some anti-psychotics.

Teens and adults with bipolar disorders may have intrusive sexual thoughts and during manic episodes may engage in sexual and other behaviors that put them at risk for bodily harm, exposure to STIs, and sexual assault. Anxiety disorders, including obsessive-compulsive thoughts and certain specific phobias, can affect interpersonal relationships and sex functioning. Those with schizophrenia spectrum disorders may have abnormal sexual concerns and obsessions. Addressing all of this is part of the sex education parents and caregivers must give the children, teens, and young adults in their care.

Depression and anxiety are sometimes a side effect of environmental pressures or events. Sexual abuse and assault can result in a trauma, depressive, or behavioral response. Some children may act out when depressed or traumatized, while others will shut down and show no emotion. Suppression of gender identity or sexual orientation may also result in a child or teen developing mental illnesses.

Having a mental illness can make relationships with others difficult in part because the person simply doesn't know how to be in a relationship. When a great deal of focus has been on the day-to-day management of the illness, education and guidance about intimate social interactions might have been overlooked. Even so, parents can assume that for the most part, children and teens still want intimate and sexual relationships and pleasure. They need parents' help and that of the professionals on your team to get adequate sex education, as well as help with navigating interpersonal relationships and knowledge of how to protect themselves from pregnancy and sexually transmitted diseases and infections.

Gender Diversity/Transgender/Sexual Orientation

Children have a wide range of interests, but cultural norms may push them to have a preference for toy, activities, or friends. In the past, children firmly nonconforming with their preferences in these areas might have been labeled as having a gender identity disorder. Children, teens or adults who expressed their identity as being the opposite of their biological sex, in other words, to be transgender, might also be placed in the category of having a mental illness. In some instances, health-care professionals and parents felt in-depth treatment was necessary to bring identity and biology into agreement.

Today, although the subject continues to be controversial, most major psychological and psychiatric organizations call for a change in attitudes and approaches to those who are gender diverse and/or transgender. Understandably, parents can be confused and experience a lot of societal pressure to "help" their child become what is viewed as gender consistent.

This situation can heavily impact the mental health of both the child and family. Children who are gender nonconforming are at risk for depression, bullying and trauma as a result of societal and family expectations and experiences. At present, parents have three choices for how to handle a nonconforming gender child: they can be gender affirmative, that is, they support the child in his or her identity; they can take a wait-and-see attitude to see if the child's behavior and identity continue or change as the child grows up; they can seek to actively suppress or discourage their child's gender identity. Better psychological outcomes result from the first two approaches; some states, such as California, have specific laws against forced treatment.

In terms of the sex education of your child, parents who are being affirmative or taking the wait-and-see approach will undoubtedly come up against the discrepancy of information in most child sex-education books (cis-gendered and heteronormative) and what your child asserts for him or herself. It will be on you to help your child understand this. You can use phrases like, "Most of the time, boys will have penises and scrotum and girls will have a vulva and vagina, but some girls might have a penis and some boys might have a vagina." Or you might try something on this order: "We accept how you see yourself, but others might be confused or don't agree. We are here to support and accept you. If someone tries to tell you that you are wrong, don't argue or fight. That person just needs more education to understand that people can be different from what they expect."

Children who are older, in the tween or teen years, might want to use different pronouns for themselves, such as "they" instead of he or she. It is important to ask and to respect the names and ways in which people want to refer to themselves. The idea is to help guide them to their own conclusions about themselves and their body/identity, as well help protect them from the opinions of others.

What often confuses parents and others is that gender identity and sexual orientation are not the same. Furthermore, regardless of gender identity, people may also identify as lesbian, gay, bisexual, or even asexual. In addition to difficulties parents may have in knowing what to include when they educate their LGBTQ children, most sex-education curricula, at least in the United States, do not include any mention of gender diversity or identity or sexual orientation. Abstinence-only focused wording refers just to marriage as husband and wife, ignoring that same-sex marriage is now legal in this country. Group-discussion questions at school or elsewhere in some areas of the US are based solely on heterosexual norms and scripts.

Parents need help knowing how to respond if their child comes out as trans or gay, and what to say about dating and navigating a mainly heterosexual world. They also need to be prepared to help their child if he or she is bullied, attacked, or shunned.

Proper sex and relationship education is vital for LGBTQ kids and teens for their health and safety. Higher rates of depression, suicide, substance abuse, and violence against them are well documented. To a great extent, much of the information parents provide is the same when it comes to things like the basics of anatomy, sexual and emotional development, consent, or protection. Some of the education may well be for parents. For example, you may have to seek other people to be on your team for information about what to do when your child comes out to you, what kind of language to use, dating tips, what to do if they are attracted to someone who is not gay or lesbian, or for other support you and they might need. You may need to get a better understanding of how people who are lesbian or gay engage in sexual pleasure and avoid stereotypes. If your child does come out to you, please respect his or her privacy and check before you share that information with others. Parent and Friends of Lesbians and Gays, known as PFLAG has support groups across the country and can assist parents. Talking with someone who has been through similar experiences can be extremely helpful.

Sexual and Physical Abuse or Assault

Although statistics show that children with disabilities and differences are much more likely to be the victims of violence, including sexual abuse and assault, the rate of violence among children and teens in the general population is also staggering. One in five girls are reported to have experienced sexual abuse as have one in 20 boys. Data from the CDC/Kaiser Permanente Adverse Childhood Experience study shows that physical abuse occurs at a higher rate than sexual abuse (28.3% vs. 20.7%, respectively), with emotional abuse, physical and emotional neglect not too far behind (10.6, 9.9, and 14.8%, respectively). Date rape or attempted rape happens to approximately one in four college-aged women. The vast majority knows the perpetrator and drugs and alcohol often play a role, having been used by both parties in well over half the cases reported.

Surprisingly, in some cases girls and women weren't sure they had been raped because they didn't know the actual definition of the term. While recent campaigns to end sexual violence have promoted an only-yes-means-yes standard to remove any possible misunderstandings about the words no or stop, proving consent or lack thereof can be difficult. This makes it especially important to talk with your child about the meaning of consent and situations where consent might be impaired. The consequences for acting otherwise can be dire for all concerned.

We also know that those who have a history of abuse, assault, or neglect have a significantly higher risk of developing a mental illness, being suicidal, abusing drugs and alcohol, and entering into violent or abusive relationships. Further, children and teens may become voluntarily sexual active at an early age, depending on the age when the abuse occurred. They are also more likely to experience sexually transmitted diseases or infection and unintended pregnancy.

If the child you are raising has experienced sexual or physical abuse, it's crucial for you to remember that this child is more than his or her experiences. Parents, foster parents, or caretakers sometimes filter everything in the child's life through the abusive experiences and may even avoid talking about sex because of fear it could be traumatic or unwanted. Instead, respect the child's privacy and ask permission to discuss what happened to them with other, appropriate people. Parents are the most important people in helping a child heal and develop healthy emotional and sexual relationships. Even therapists trained in treating trauma may have their own issues regarding sexuality; some may not have adequate training to bring aspects of healthy sexuality and relationships into their treatment, concentrating only on a reduction or remission of trauma symptoms without going further.

Discovering that your child has been abused or maltreated can be traumatizing for parents. In this case I would urge parents to seek help for themselves, which will enable them to be there for their children. It's not easy, but parents are the ones the child lives with each day and healing is a day-by-day journey.

An even more challenging situation for parents is when children who have been abused or assaulted engage in those behaviors with other children or act out sexually in some other way. Professional help is critical to help address this; our culture has a strident view of sexual behavior of and between children. It has been my very sad experience in clinical practice to see children labeled as sex offenders when they are acting out of their own trauma and experiences. Just some of the important topics to discuss with children include boundaries, consent, touch, nudity, privacy, safety, and respect. Address the issue of masturbation as a self-soothing behavior the way you would with any child, with an emphasis on privacy. However, it's wise to expand the concept of self-soothing to other practices for your child so the attention isn't mostly on physical pleasure.

Children and teens continue to need touch and closeness, but these may evoke different responses in them. For example, young children may become overly clingy and touch adults inappropriately at times. The way to handle this is as you would with children who do not have a history of abuse; teach them again about boundaries. Your child might freeze while getting a hug or other kind of physical affection or even when you bring up the topic of sex. Don't ignore the response. Calmly let him or her know that this response is okay and that you are there for support. Young children may not be able to verbalize what is happening and that is okay too. Just being present for them can be a big help. It can be extremely helpful for teens and young adults to know ahead of time that they might freeze when they are voluntarily being emotionally or sexually close to another person, no matter how safe they think that person is. The biggest goal is to not only help children heal, but to give them the chance to develop healthy emotional and sexual relationships.

And What about You?

Teaching children and teens about sex and relationships is a big part of parenting in the best of times, but it becomes even more challenging when children have medical or psychological/ developmental/ societal issues. It is crucial that as parents you remember to take care of yourselves first so that you will be able to give to others in your lives.

The resources I've listed in the following will be a good start for you to increase your knowledge base and explore your attitudes and values. Connecting to other parents and professionals can be helpful and go a long way toward reducing the isolation or stigma you might feel. Empowering children through education and advocacy will help make their lives richer and will increase their safety. Keep in mind that this isn't about being perfect; it's about doing what all parents can do – your best.

Resources

General Websites

Advocates for Youth

http://www.advocatesforyouth.org/publications/publications-a-z/479-sex-education-for-physically-emotionally-and-mentally-challenged-youth

This website is one of the best; it is all about sex education and has a specific section for educating youth with physical, emotional, and mental challenges.

Center for Parent Information and Resources

http://www.parentcenterhub.org/?s=sex+education

In addition to offering a variety of resources for parents and teachers of children with intellectual disabilities, the site has information specifically on sex education. There are materials available for specific disabilities such as Autism Spectrum Disorders (ASD), cerebral palsy, deaf-blindness, intellectual disabilities, learning disabilities, and spina bifada, to name a few.

Susan's Sex Support Site

http://www.sexsupport.org/SexEd.html

A site with many resources, including links to various books and websites, as well as a sex support forum.

Developmental/Intellectual Disabilities (ASD, MR)

Sex and U

http://www.sexualityandu.ca/teachers/teaching-sex-ed-for-youth-with-intellectual-disabilities

From Canada, and available in French and English, this site has basic information about sex and development, lesson plans, and how to manage controversy about educating your child.

Sexuality Education for Children and Adolescents with Autism Spectrum Disorders

https://www.kennedykrieger.org/sites/default/files/event files/card-sexuality-talk.pdf

This pdf by Laura Solomon, PsyD is an excellent overview of the reasons for sex education for ASD children, what parents fear, and specific examples of what to cover and how to do so in a way your child can understand.

The Arc

http://www.thearc.org/what-we-do/resources/fact-sheets/sexual-offenses

This website has a page regarding intellectual disability and sexual offenses. Parents who are aware of common problems for children and adults with intellectual disabilities are better prepared to help them avoid legal problems while still empowering them to have a sex-positive approach to life.

Visual Impairments/Blindness

Wonderbaby.org

http://www.wonderbaby.org/articles/teaching-your-blind-child-about-sexuality

Funded by Perkins School for the Blind, this site has many resources for parents of children with visual impairments.

Texas School for the Blind and Visually Impaired

http://www.tsbvi.edu/science/203-resources/3253-sexuality-education-for-children-with-visual-impairments-a-parents-guide

An excellent page with all kinds of resources for parents, including a parent's guide to sex education.

Deaf/Hard of Hearing

Resource List

http://documents.nationaldb.org/products/webinar/Soc-Skills%20SexEd%20Teaching%20Resource%20List.pdf

A pdf with a list of resources for social skills and sex education geared toward those with sensory disabilities.

ASL Signs for Sexuality

https://www.youtube.com/watch?v=Fk6oaREO3dA

This is part one of a YouTube series to teach basic signs for sexuality and relationships. There are other videos available to assist you in teaching your child sexual anatomy, medical terms, etc.

Physical Disabilities and Chronic Illness/Mental Illness

United Cerebral Palsy

http://ucp.org/resources/health-and-wellness/sexuality/

A website devoted to the advancement of "life without limits" for people with any disability; it includes a special section devoted to sexuality education for parents and professionals.

University of Michigan Health System

http://www.med.umich.edu/yourchild/topics/disabsex.htm

This page has a resource list and contains the 2006 policy statement from the American Academy of Pediatrics regarding sexuality of children with developmental disabilities.

Gender Diversity/Sexual Orientation

Gender Spectrum

https://www.genderspectrum.org/explore-topics/parenting-and-family/

Gender Spectrum is a site dedicated to providing assistance and support for all children and teens of gender diversity. It has a specific section for parenting and family, as well as sections for teens, regarding the education system, one aimed toward medical professionals who might work with gender diverse youth, and an area for mental health professionals. Social service resources and legal aspects of being gender-expansive are available, as is a section for faith and spiritual leaders.

American Psychological Association

http://www.apadivisions.org/division-44/resources/advocacy/transgender-children.pdf

This links to a fact sheet produced by the APA to help people understand what gender diversity and transgender identity means in children. It is designed to help parents understand their child or other children better and give them some language to use when talking with others their child's life.

Gender Now Coloring Book: A learning Adventure for Children and Adults** (2010) **by Maya Gonzalez and Matthew Smith-Gonzalez

Published in 2010, this book is to help children and parents explore gender expression. It is appropriate whether or not your child is expressing gender variance, and it is an excellent resource for all parents and groups who want to help children learn to be accepting and connected to others.

Advocates for Youth

http://www.advocatesforyouth.org/parents/173-parents

This resource, listed in a previous chapter, is the go-to resource for parents of LGBT children.

Sexual, Physical, and Emotional Abuse/Assault and Neglect

A Trauma Informed Approach for Adolescent Sexual Health by Joann Schlade, M.S., L.M.F.T.

http://resourcesforresolvingviolence.com/wp-content/uploads/A-Trauma-Informed-Approach-for-Adolescent-Sexual-Health.pdf

For parents and professional alike, this 2012 pdf addresses how to approach sex education for youth who have experienced different types of trauma.

About the Author

Lin Myers Jovanović, PhD, earned her doctorate in Medical Psychology at the Uniformed Services University of the Health Sciences, Bethesda, MD. After postdoctoral training at Stanford University and University of California, San Francisco, she became a professor at California State University, Stanislaus, where she has been on the faculty for over 28 years. Through her research, teaching, clinical work, and community workshops, she has been committed to the field of sexology.

Myers Jovanović is a member of the International Academy of Sex Research and the Society for Sex Therapists and Researchers. She serves on the editorial board of the Archives of Sexual Behavior and also reviews for Journal of Sex Research. In her private practice her specialties include couples counseling and sex therapy (see **www.relationship-explorations.com**), as well as providing parent coaching and giving speeches around the country (see **www.plainspokenparenting.com**).

She lives with her husband in Grass Valley, CA, and is the mother of three daughters and one son, and grandmother of five.

If this book was helpful to you, please consider leaving a reader review on the author's Amazon page. It would be very much appreciated! You can find her page at: http://www.amazon.com/books. Dr. Jovanović would love to hear from you about your experience with this book and its material. Contact her at: **www.plainspokenparenting.com**.

CPSIA information can be obtained
at www.ICGtesting.com
Printed in the USA
LVOW10s0322060717
540367LV00015B/186/P

9 780997 863505